WITHDRAWN

Big Rigs
& Elvis
The Grand
Dragon Wayne

new essays
by Michael Perry

ISBN: 0-9631695-6-4

Address all editorial correspondence
and orders for additional copies of this book to

Whistlers and Jugglers Press
P.O. Box 1346
Eau Claire, WI 54702-1346

Web site: <www.sneezingcow.com>

e-mail correspondence and inquiries:
<mikperry@win.bright.net>

PRINTED IN THE UNITED STATES OF AMERICA
First Printing   11/99   5C
Second Printing   1/03   1M

cover design:
KZen Design & Graphics
644 Twenty-First Street, Chetek, WI 54728
Phone: (715) 924-3025 • Fax: (715) 924-3838
e-mail: <KZen@discover-net.net>

book design and text layout:
Frank Smoot
e-mail: <c.landis@innocent.com>

► Credits and Permissions

"Anatomy of an Interview" originally appeared in the September-October 1998 issue of *No Depression*.

"Convoy" originally appeared as "The Truck Driver" in the April 1999 issue of *ICON*.

At press time, "Falling Together" was scheduled for publication in *Salon*.

"Farther Along: A Eulogy for Grandpa Jones" originally appeared as a "Farther Along" column in the May-June 1998 issue of *No Depression*.

"Fear This" originally appeared in the Fall 1997 issue of *Troika*; it was subsequently reprinted as "Bumper-Sticker Bravado" in the March-April 1998 issue of the *Utne Reader*.

"The Haul Road" originally appeared in the January-February 1999 issue of *Road King*.

"Insoluble Toxins" was originally contracted for publication in *Poets & Writers Magazine*; at press time, Magnuson was two books down the line and *P & W* still owed me a whopping two-figure kill fee. In a slow-motion fit of pique, I have allowed my subscription to lapse.

"The Osmotic Elvis" originally appeared as "The Unshakeable Elvis" in the August 1997 issue of *The World & I*; the version within is reprinted with permission from *The World & I* magazine, a publication of the Washington Times Corporation.

"A Pilgrim's Progress" originally appeared in the July-August 1999 issue of *No Depression*.

"Put the Wet Stuff on the Red Stuff" originally appeared in the April 1999 issue of *Esquire*.

"Ramblin' Jack Elliott" originally appeared as "On The Road" in the March-April 1998 issue of *No Depression*.

"The Road Ahead: Life of the American Trucker" originally appeared in the January 1999 issue of *The World & I*; the version within is reprinted with permission from *The World & I* magazine, a publication of the Washington Times Corporation.

"The Road Gang" originally appeared as a "Screen Door" column in the July-August 1997 issue of *No Depression*.

"Rolling Thunder" originally appeared in the July-August 1998 issue of *Road King*.

"RSVP to the KKK" originally appeared as "RSVP to a Racist" in the Summer 1998 issue of *Troika*.

▶ Contents

Preface | 6

Swelter | 9
Scarlet Ribbons | 12
You Are Here | 17
Put the Wet Stuff on the Red Stuff | 25
Falling Together | 33
What We Want | 37
RSVP to the KKK | 42
Fear This | 47
The Haul Road | 50
The Road Gang | 57
Convoy | 60
Rolling Thunder | 70
A Pilgrim's Progress | 74
Farther Along: A Eulogy for Grandpa Jones | 84
The Osmotic Elvis | 88
Ramblin' Jack Elliott | 96
Anatomy of an Interview | 104
Insoluble Toxins | 114
The Road Ahead: Life of the American Trucker | 125
Branding God | 133

About the Author | 149

▶ Preface

I recently traveled to a school on the western edge of Wisconsin to speak with several groups of grade schoolers about writing. Upon my arrival, I was informed that over the noon hour, I would be taken down the road to eat pizza with a select group of children who had won a writing contest. Part of their prize — I certainly hope there was more, or they'll be off writing contests for life — was lunch with me. This was a small, rural town, and as a result, the "restaurant" was actually a collection of four tables and three booths tucked in the back corner of a gas station and convenience store. When I arrived, the children were already in place. As I navigated through stacks of motor oil and racks of Fritos, their teacher spotted me.

A word about this teacher: She was a wonderful woman, dedicated and sincere, keen to invigorate the children to learn beyond the walls of the classroom, and beyond that, had seen fit to hire me for the day, something which always leaves me nonplussed and deeply grateful. I thank her now as I thanked her then. Nonetheless, as I rounded the Little Debbie display, I cringed as she leapt to her feet and announced, "Here comes the author, children!"

I could see heads swiveling all along the range of my peripheral vision. I ducked my head.

"Hello, author!" she sang.

I pulled one of those ghastly dog-caught-in-the-cat-food grins. My ears glowed like a matched pair of overripe beets.

"Children, the author has come to share his wisdom with us!"

I shot a glance to the rear, gauging the possibility of retreat. I figured I could slide behind the beef jerky display, hurdle the motor oil, and be down the highway before the final echoes of this latest encomium finished ringing around the milk case. But I knew I had to stay the course. I owed it to the children. I owed it to art. I owed it to the fact that it was a paying gig. And so I pressed forward, aware now that every eye in the place was on me, feeling for all the world as if I had skipped into a logger's convention wearing a spiff pink tutu.

The cash register had stopped ringing.

About this time, I noticed two men in one of the booths. They had the look of father and son, about 50 and 30. Although it was still early spring, they were well-tanned and coated with a fine dust, and had no doubt come straight from the fields. They'd been looking at me sideways ever since the teacher's first hallelujah, but when she announced that I would shortly be dispensing wisdom, the older man gave the slightest little snort. The teacher, no doubt tuned to snort frequency by vocation, turned on him, not in anger, but in joy.

"But Sir!" she caroled. "He is an *author*."

His gaze was pure chilled steel. His voice was of similar extrusion. "I," he said, "am a *farmer*."

For the record, I'm on his side.

Cussedness — a note regarding profanity

Excepting incidents involving intransigent computer software or incoming gunfire, I was raised to eschew swear words, and largely do. But throughout my desperately slow, utterly tenuous, and raggedly incomplete development as a writer, I have perhaps learned one thing: *try for rhythm and truth*. Profanity frequently serves both. And so, you'll find a little here and there in these pages. Considering the surfeit of relative and literal profanities ping-ponging about our contemporary milieu, one feels a bit goofy speaking apologetically about such a thing, but: a) anyone familiar with that portion of my work consisting of frisky little humoresques and soft-focus nature rhapsodies won't be expecting naughty words, and I don't want them to pop up unnannounced like a bug in the salad; and, b) anyone who knows my mother would never expect her son to use such language. ◄

▶ Swelter

I was young when the streaking fad hit. Mid-grade school, maybe. Sinful, I thought. But I had a go at it. Dropping our clothes beside the sinkhole in the sheep pasture, a friend and I took off across the field, chasing his horse, Daisy. Daisy had been trained for the circus. You could vault to her back from behind. We never tried that with our clothes off.

It seems ludicrous now, the image of two hairless children capering through the fat alfalfa, forty acres from the nearest road, with no one to see us but my younger brother. Even then more sensible than I, he sat at the edge of the sinkhole, nibbling a bird-legged stem of canary grass. He knew we weren't raised that way. And we weren't. So after a lap or two, my friend and I put on our jeans, adjusted our t-shirts to our tan-lines, and ascended the lower limbs of popple trees, jackknives open, to mark the day in the bitter bark. I haven't disrobed in public since.

But I know why we stripped that day.

Blame summer.

Summer is a seducer. After bundling through another tight-lipped winter, after enduring the mounting frustration of spring's titillating dance of veils, we gape as summer comes sliding down her blazing ecliptic like a woman down a bannister. She laughs with her head thrown far back; she throws her hands high in the air, releasing fistfuls of butterflies. She belly-dances through the cornfields until the dust rises like a charmed snake, hanging in fat curls, leaving you cotton-mouthed. She makes the fox pant, she drives the hawk to thin air. Weaker creatures curtain themselves away to complain.

"Can't stand this," say people who only months ago chattered and whined in the cold. "It's not so much the heat. . . ," they mewl, their humidifiers sagging and worn to a frazzle, tattered after cranking out a ceaseless fog against winter's moistureless air.

Give me summer. Give me dappled cattails sashaying under a breeze so like hot breath it stirs unclean thoughts; give me warm ditches all clotted with frog eggs, sunning turtles, wheezing nights. In the summer we live dangerously, driving fast with our vulnerable elbows out the window. We loosen our clothes, make love with the screens open. Summer makes us fearless. One summer I was 1200 miles from home. I wrote a brave letter to a girl I didn't know. When I returned, a few hot days of August remained. Beneath a moth-clogged porch light, she took my face in her hands and kissed me.

In the summer, sweat is easily earned, rising at the slightest provocation. In the haymow, alfalfa chaff with the scent of toasted tea plasters at the hollow of a farmer's neck; his forearms ripple shiny and green. Over dishes in the kitchen, his wife turns her wrist, runs it across her brow.

Summer taunts the weak. Morning glories rise early like pious old women to prayer, pale purple and cool to the touch. But by midmorning faith fails them; they purse their lips and retire frowning to their clinging vines. In the meantime, summer has taken over the day, driving sheep to shade. Sparrows wallow in the dust, and horses stand wide-legged and motionless, heads down. She has built a heavy heat, summer, a heat with momentum. Momentum to carry well into the night, where it will pad the air, squat above the sheets, dim the stars.

Like any decadent creature, summer shows her age prematurely. As early as July the greens assume a harder edge. Blight stains the popple leaves, the timothy grows stalky and thin. Like a thickening woman, one halter top strap off the shoulder, like a man adjusting his thin hair while his sports car idles, there is evidence that summer is going to seed, leaving you to nurse regret through the fall, the season of penitence.

Fall is penitence. Winter is abstinence. But the cycle is a circle, and fasting sharpens hunger. By springtime, you are ready to sin again. And summer will oblige you, whistling like a torch, flaming and shameless, with the power to make young boys strip naked and dance for the sun.

We grew apart, my streaking friend and I. He graduated, and a year later, I left town. There were rumors of trouble, then rumors of his being born again. One humid day a year ago, I drove by his house and there was nothing out front but a rusty truck. His windows were tightly shut. I thought it symbolic: Summer, heavily made up and waiting in the yard; him having none of it. I was overreaching, of course, imposing metaphor to serve my own purpose. It turns out he runs a business reclaiming concrete silos — exhausting, dangerous work performed high above barnyards. While I hunker beneath a roof, rearranging words in an attempt to capture summer, bring it inside, he is out in it, the sun hot on his bare back, baking him like the unpicked stones in the fields below.

We ran into each other at the local gas station recently. He tossed a carton of cigarettes through his truck window and came over to talk. We caught up a bit, him with his sunburned, work-skinned arms folded across the front of a sleeveless t-shirt, me in my clean jeans. I didn't bring up the streaking, didn't ask him to comment on my attempts to characterize summer as sensuous seducer. He did mention that he sometimes travels to South America in the winter. He didn't say why. I'd like to think summer draws him down there. The temptress, that sort of thing. But I suspect he has other reasons, and another metaphor withers.

And so in the end, summer is simply warm weather. For all this pungent talk of sweat and seduction, I believe summer is understood only by the child too young to be troubled by the adult inferences of nakedness and heat, unfettered by metaphor and allusion, content simply to sprint through the grass and get about this business of growing old under the sun. ◄

▶ Scarlet Ribbons

The man in the small room with me is a convicted murderer. He is immense and simple, looks as if he was raised on potatoes and homemade biscuits. I'd lay money that before he wound up here, his clothes smelled of bacon grease. He knows I am uneasy. I know he knows, because he looked me square in the eye, grinned, and told me so. Still, *The New York Times Magazine* has given me an assignment, and although I may be edgy in this prison, in this room with concrete blocks close all around, with this bulky killer two feet away, I must complete it.

I am to determine if the prisoner is happy.

The first person to whom I ever administered an intramuscular injection was a cheery wee granny. I see her still, seated on a hospital chair, flannel gown hiked up to expose her left quadriceps, head fluffed with a blessing of fine white curls, smile as sweet and warm as a batch of sugar cookies. The steel needle is cocked an inch from her skin, and she chirps: "Have you ever done this before?"

"Oh yes," I lie. Brightly. Smoothly. Never breaking eye contact.

Heraclitus said you can never step in the same river twice. Jorge Luis Borges said time is forever dividing itself toward innumerable futures — that we choose one alternative at the expense of all others. We can never be who we set out to be, but will always be who we were. I went to college to become a nurse. I became a writer. We spring from a thicket of tangents. I remember the exact moment I decided to become a nurse. I was reading *Sports Illustrated* in the high school library. I was supposed to be in World

Literature, but the university recruiter was in town, and we were allowed to skip class to catch her pitch. I signed up, but once in the library, headed straight for the magazine rack, lolling through *People* and *Newsweek* while the rest of the students joined the recruiter at a long table. Late in her presentation, I overheard her reciting a list of majors: "Biology. Business. Economics. History. Nursing."

"*Nursing*," I thought. "That sounds interesting."

I filled out the necessary paperwork, and reported for class in the fall.

Nursing is so easily caricatured by white skirts and chilly bed pans. Pills and needles. Shots. But this is like saying painting is about paint. Practiced at its best, nursing is humane art, arisen from intimate observation and expressed through care. Again and again our instructors reminded us that every patient is a point of convergence, an intersection of body, mind, and spirit. We were trained to obtain quantifiable data with stethoscopes and sphygmomanometers, but we were also warned not to ignore intuition. We learned to change sheets without removing a bedridden patient, we learned how to prevent decubitus ulcers by monitoring pressure points, we learned to stick lubricated feeding tubes up noses, but we also learned to seek eye contact, percept nonverbal communication, and establish trust so rapidly that within five minutes of meeting a stranger we could quite comfortably inquire after his bowel habits. Facilitate, reflect, and clarify; employ empathic response. These are the interviewing tools of the nurse. Also eminently functional, as it turns out, in the service of interviewing murderers for *The New York Times*. Every time I filled a syringe, I was filling my writer's pen with ink.

Heraclitus also said we are never being, but becoming, and in between clinical rotations and classes on skin disease, all nursing students were required to enroll in humanity courses. This rankled

me. I have never been taken with the concept of a liberal arts education. The idea of lounging around dissecting *Tom Jones* when I
should have been dissecting piglets always struck me as mark-
time dawdling along the road to employability. I'd change out of
surgical scrubs and hustle off to badminton class, Econ 110, or
The United States Since 1877, or Introduction to Film, or Introduction to Creative Writing, or Folk Music in America. I expected
the Chemistry 210, the General Zoology, the Developmental Psych
and the Survey of Biochemistry, and willingly submitted to the
Minnesota Multiphasic Personality Inventory assessment designed
to reassure the beehived matron at the helm of the nursing school
that I was unlikely to bite my patients or develop perverse affec-
tions for iodine swabs, but a .5 credit course in relaxation? What
did these things have to do with nursing? Peering into the thicket
of tangents, I saw nothing but obstruction.

Early one morning during a summer O.R. rotation, long before
most people had finished their first cup of coffee, a surgeon in-
flated and deflated a lung for me. It pressed out of the patient's
bisected chest like a greasy trick balloon, then shrunk back and
retreated into a cheesy lump beside the patient's writhing heart.
The mechanics were fascinating. Here was the corporeal gristle
revealed. We tote our organs around not even knowing them. There
is nothing abstract about a glistening length of intestine. But by
drawing back the curtain, the surgeon managed to reframe the
mystery. Now that I had peeked behind the liver, eyed the discrete
lumps of organ, I wondered where the spirit might lie. It's one
thing to speak of the heart as a center of emotion, quite another to
see it lurching between the lungs like a spasmodic grey slug. We
were as deep in the body as you can get — exactly where did they
keep the soul? The finite, meaty nature of it all blunted my ability
to imagine the body as a place for spirits.

When I was a child, my father, a quietly eccentric farmer, would sometimes come in the house after the evening milking, rustle up his blighted trumpet, and play "A Trumpeter's Lullaby." We sat at his feet, and he swayed above us, an overalled gnome, eyes closed, gently triple-tonguing the wistful passages. The notes twined from the brass bell in liquescent amber, settling over our hearts and shoulders, wreathing us in warm, golden light. Many years later I found myself standing at a meds cart in a surgical ward, sorting pills into cups, chafing in my polyester student nurse smock, short of sleep and overwhelmed by my patient care assignments, desperately trying to sort out the drug interactions before my instructor arrived to grill me on the same, when "A Trumpeter's Lullaby" came seeping from the speaker in the ceiling. I was swept with a desperate melancholy. I have never been so lonely. And try as I might, I could not see how the path on which I stood could be backtracked to the feet of my trumpeting father. In more dramatic circumstances, I might have stripped off my smock, gobbled the meds, and run off to join an agrarian brass band, but my instructor appeared and began to ask me if there was any danger in administering Diazepam and Clonidine in tandem. I fidgeted, answered hopefully, and resumed forward motion.

After four years, I took my nursing boards, convinced I'd fail, and passed just fine. Worked as a nurse for a while and liked it. But I kept having trouble remembering all the numbers, and how Demerol interacted with Elavil, and just what it was phagocytes did, and yet I could remember the poem the stunted guy behind me in creative writing wrote about electrical highlines, and what the professor said it lacked, and how I believed the highline guy could have done better, and how I remembered the way the folk music professor crossed his legs and fingered his guitar when he explained that the scarlet ribbons in "Scarlet Ribbons" weren't ribbons at all, but bright blood on a child's fractured head, and I thought of the lung puffing and falling, and I said if I can conjure these things so easily while I stumble over drug interactions and hematocrits, perhaps I ought to write instead. I took to talking about this. Over-frequently, apparently, because one day my girlfriend said, "Why don't you stop talking about it and do it?"

And so I did.

There was much to learn, but much less to unlearn.

I wonder if Heraclitus would dare tell the prisoner he was not stepping in the same river twice. A lifetime of days between those tan concrete blocks? Sounds like the same old river to me. Still, our little visit must have been a diversion. I imagine he chuckled with his roomie later when he described catching me in my unease. It was a fair cop. But as he leaned in and grinned, I slid the needle in and drew out what I needed. When I stepped out of the prison, it was cold and windy, but the waning light seemed to propose an answer. ◄

▶ You Are Here

Any pilot who has gone off course while "flying on visuals" knows what it is to dip from the clouds to reconnoiter the earth. To search for an orienting feature in the landscape below, a landmark that says, "You Are Here." Imagine then, how welcome the sight of a water tower, standing out like a giant pushpin stuck in a topographical map, clearly labeled with the name of the community arranged about its base.

We most commonly see water towers from ground level, often while traveling, but they are no less a source of orientation to us than they are to the pilot. From the perspective of the road, a water tower becomes a giant signpost representing a community. "Here we are," say the residents of Richmond, Indiana, all day and all night, thanks to their illuminated roadside tower. "Here we are," say the residents of Beebe, Arkansas, adding in painted epigraph, "Your Dream Hometown." Here we are, in spite of everything, declared Florida City, Florida, in 1992, after Hurricane Andrew peeled the "F" and "C" from the silver skin of their water tower, but failed to topple it. Here we are, if you look closely, says the water storage tank in Bedminster, New Jersey, its walls camouflaged with trees in silhouette.

Even when the road you travel is cybernetic, many of the towns you approach choose to introduce themselves via their water towers. Journey to the Hartington, Nebraska, web page and you'll see a simple, captionless photo of its colorful tower, looking overdressed and lonely on a plain. Denison, Iowa, presents a thumbnail photo of its million-gallon tower, and explains that the painted caption, "It's a Wonderful Life," is in honor of Denison native Donna Reed for her most famous film appearance. Go north of the border to

Red Deer, Alberta, Canada, select the water tower page, and while no picture pops up, you will be able to learn from the text that the tower is "big" and "green." Moreover, "you may be interested to know that the water tower has never leaked." Knoxville, Illinois, shares a photo and the information that the water in its tower is "naturally fluoridated and slightly radioactive."

"Here we are," say water towers on behalf of a community, "and this says something about us."

My hometown water tower stands just off Main Street, along the soft descent leading from the freeway overpass to the old, underfed highway at the center of town. Built in a style the experts refer to as "double ellipsoidal multicolumn," it exhibits a solid stance, the four slim legs angling outward a bit as they drop from their attachment at the convex belly of the silver-gray tank. Simple block letters, spare and black, follow the curvature of the sidewalls, peeking from behind the wraparound catwalk: NEW AUBURN. The cap, a meniscus of steel, is crowned with a small American flag. During the holiday season, a star of lights joins the flag. A black-and-white picture of the the tower, taken shortly after its construction in 1950, hangs in the village hall. It might have been taken yesterday. When I roll up the exit ramp from the freeway, I enjoy the thought of people approaching town back when the old highway was in its heyday, seeing the same water tower, albeit from the opposite direction. More than the houses, more than the streets, more than the small green sign at the outskirts, it has always been the sight of the water tower that has told us, "here you are."

No less an authority on American culture than Garrison Keillor has reinforced the image of water tower as icon. Winners of *A Prairie Home Companion*'s "Talent from Towns Under 2000" contest tote home a trophy modeled after the witch-hatted steel towers that dot Minnesota's plains. Keillor himself chose the image, and sees it as symbolic of small-town America.

Keillor's frame of reference is Midwestern, and that frame of reference is telling. For someone raised in the heartland, it's easy to think of the old silver water tower as definitively iconic. Of course, this is not so. In Ypsilanti, Michigan, water has been stored since 1891 in a 147-foot-tall stone and concrete tower. A tower standing in Coral Gables, Florida, is disguised as a lighthouse of Spanish-Moorish architectural extraction, with a sundial attached to its south face. In Mendocino, California, a tower constructed in 1857 to serve the Carlson City Hotel still stands. Constructed of redwood, it has the appearance of a tall rectangular box, capped with a flat pyramid of shake shingles. In 1870, the hotel was destroyed by fire, but the tower endured. One year later, the Chicago Water Tower survived the Great Chicago Fire. Constructed of limestone in a style referred to as "naïvely Gothic," the tower includes turrets, battlements, and slit windows with architraves. Topping it all off is a green copper cap. In 1969, the American Water Works Association chose the Chicago Water Tower as its inaugural American Water Landmark. Consequently, one of the first water towers officially designated as classic had no legs; it was crenelated, not witch-hatted.

In 1895, Jacob Miller built a limestone water tower in Clinton, Wisconsin. The tank was made of wood; when fluctuations in the weather caused leaks, residents turned out to hand-tighten the turnbuckles. Wooden tanks were still being constructed in the 1950s; you're most likely to spot one in New York, Philadelphia, and on the Chicago skyline. Early steel towers were patched together with riveted panels. But by 1930, welding had replaced riveting.

The smooth surface of welded tanks is easier to maintain, and welding allows a versatility of design not possible with riveted construction. The intricate detailing of the 100,000 gallon pineapple that stood atop the Dole Cannery in Honolulu until it was dismantled in 1993 is all the more remarkable for the fact that Chicago Bridge and Iron constructed it in 1927, using the riveting method.

Today, water storage vessels are classified in three configurations: reservoirs, standpipes and elevated tanks. A reservoir is generally a tank with a diameter greater than its height. Relative simplicity of design keeps fabrication costs low; however, reservoirs must be constructed on high ground if water is to flow by gravity.

A standpipe is defined as a tank that rests on the ground but has a height greater than its diameter; in other words, if a reservoir is a tuna can, a standpipe is a pop can. The extra height is used to create pressure for water distribution. The oldest steel standpipe in continuous use is located in Dedham, Massachussetts. Built in 1881, the Dedham tank tops the Steel Plate Fabricators Association's "Century Club," a list of 22 steel water storage tanks that have been been in continuous service for over 100 years.

Elevated tanks — true water towers — are subclassified by style and capacity. In addition to the double ellipsoidal version that stands in my town, two other common variations include spherical single pedestal tanks (the ones that resemble giant mushrooms) and fluted column tanks, featuring a broad, fluted central support column beneath a tank shaped like an aspirin tablet.

There are deviations from the standards. Gaffney, South Carolina, promotes the peach trade with the "Peachoid," a million-gallon peach-shaped tower replete with 12-foot stem, 60-foot leaf, sculptured cleft, and even a peachy little nipple. Built by the Chicago Bridge and Iron Company and painted by artist Peter Freudenburg, the Peachoid has its own website, and has even been touched by scandal (owing to the remarkable resemblance of another town's copycat tower). A water tower in Plant City, Florida, is shaped like a giant strawberry. Another in Germantown, Maryland, is a spherical simulacrum of the earth viewed from space. Water towers have been constructed in the shape of apples, milk bottles, ketchup bottles, baby food jars, Dixie Cups, Mickey Mouse, a cake with candles. A giant coffee percolator in Stanton, Iowa, honors hometown girl Virginia Christine, the Mrs. Olson of Folgers coffee fame. More than one country club has erected a water tower painted to look like a golf ball perched on a tee.

But of course, no matter the shape, the color, or the message, a water tower's first purpose is to store water. Or, more specifically, to store energy: Pump stations along the line repressurize larger water systems, but in smaller systems, gravity alone forces water through the pipes. And so, in my town, the nearer your tap to the tower, the less time it takes to top off your teapot.

A tower also equalizes supply and demand. During peak water use — generally between 6:00 p.m. and 10:00 p.m. — demand may outstrip pumping capacities. The difference can be made up from storage. Then, when demand drops below average — generally from 10:00 p.m. to 7:00 a.m. — reserves are replenished. The ability to draw from reserves also allows your town to save money by running pumps during off-peak electricity demand periods, when power is cheaper. And storage reserves are essential in the event of a fire, when firefighting efforts can rapidly exceed normal peak demands.

Have you ever closed a tap abruptly and heard the water pipes clunk? That's "water hammer." Water hammer occurs when pumps switch on and off, or valves open or close. Surprisingly powerful pressure surges result, and can seriously damage pipes and equipment. Water towers help offset water hammer damage, channeling the surges up the riser, where it is absorbed in the tank.

There is, in America, a cultural *corps d'elite* of sorts, a fraternity salted throughout the generations, the members of which, likely near the age of their emancipation, took a trip to the top of the town water tower. Most carried paint and left behind the classic "Class of . . ." inscription. Others, in the process of declaring undying love, foresight clouded by infatuation and euphoric *chutz-*

pah, left behind incriminating initials. A recent initiate (or team of initiates) in Archer City, Texas, eschewed tradition to address current events. After city officials spent $13,000 to repaint the water tower, they invested an additional $1,000 to install flat steel bars on the tower legs to thwart upwardly mobile graffiti artists. "Now," said a city representative, "if any kids climb up there, we're going to give them a spanking."

Shortly thereafter, the tank's defenses proved pregnable. The latest graffito? *You must give us a spanking.*

Arnie Napiwocki may have the answer to Archer City's problems. He is the owner of Lane Tank Company of Mosinee, Wisconsin. Much of his time is spent repainting water towers. It's an esoteric profession. "People who do elevated tank work are rare," he says. "Insurance is so expensive. . . . Workman's comp is way, way up there." In 1889, when construction workers were erecting a 147-foot tower in Ypsilanti, they invested in their own form of insurance by incorporating three crosses, still visible today, into the design.

Napiwocki's professional knowledge is laced with arcana: "Ambient air quality laws stipulate no one may put more than 5.7 pounds of dust into the air without a permit. The official definition of dust is any airborne material. That means if I drop a six-pound rock off your water tank, I'm in violation." It also means that prior to sandblasting paint containing hazardous compounds, he must wrap the entire tank in a tent — Christo has nothing on Napiwocki. He knows a tank must be emptied before he paints it. "Otherwise they sweat constantly."

He knows better than to emblazon a tank with "1996 State Football Champs" without a word of caution. "What about next year, when the girls volleyball team wins? And then the golf team? It can get expensive, and usually you're dealing with taxpayer money. Sometimes they're better off to just put up a sign."

And Napiwocki knows a thing or two about water tower graffiti. "It runs in cycles," he says. "Once it starts, it continues until the town cracks down." One of Napiwocki's regular customers, a small town in northern Wisconsin, recently suffered a rash of graffiti postings and hired Napiwocki to put obstructive gear at the base of the tower. "These kids rode by while we were putting the stuff up and said, 'We're going up there anyway.' I told them, 'Listen, this is costing your town a lot of money. Next time you go up there, just hang a banner.

"A month later, the town called. They wanted me to come take a banner down."

Once a day, Rob, the village maintenance man in New Auburn, opens the door to a tiny brick hut at the base of the water tower. The interior is clean as a kitchen. Standing beside an electric pump motor the size of a pig, he takes the pulse of the system, checks dials and gauges, and makes notes in a log. In the winter, he will be especially careful to check the condition of the circulating pump. If it fails unnoticed, a giant "ice doughnut" will form at the top of the tank. Come spring, it will shift and rip the steel as if it were tinfoil.

Twice a year, Rob climbs the tower to replace the flag. On his most recent ascent, the village board gave me permission to climb with him. What I saw surprised me. There was the old feed mill, there was the fire hall, there were our eleven streets: But this wasn't the town I thought I'd see. It appeared smaller — as if it could be gathered up in an armful - and yet at once more spacious. It seemed no distance at all from the tower to the implement store at the northern outskirts, and yet, cramped yards that can be crossed in twenty steps looked roomy and wide. There were sounds: the grating trundle of a child rolling down a driveway on a Big Wheel, a rumbling load of channel iron being trailered down Main Street, two women in backyard conversation, the yap of a dog, a table saw.

I circled the catwalk twice. Rob had already finished hanging the flag, and it was time to descend. Looking to the blue hills
in the distance, I misstepped and leaned instinctively into the dense
bulk of the tank. It felt cool, deeply solid. I thought of all this
water, 50,000, gallons, 47 or so gallons of which — based on my
water bills to date — I would draw before the day was over. Water
is life, and, as far as this town is concerned, this is the source.
This tank, with its unseen pulse, its cycles of filling and emptying,
is our communal heart, and threaded through the ground beneath
us, to all edges of the place we live, are the vessels, the arteries
from which we tap our own little daily portion.

Today, when I pass the tower and look to the catwalk, I think
of what I saw from that place above the ground but beneath the
sky, and understand: *You are here.* ◄

▶ Put the Wet Stuff on the Red Stuff

The spring, the fall, I don't remember — I just recall that it was one of those brown days, leached and barren with cold. The fire phone rang, its unbroken jangle like a logging chain slung down a coal chute, and the siren on the water tower sawed into the air as it does every day at noon and nine, only this time twice, so anyone working outside would know it was a fire. When we converged at the fire hall, there were exactly four of us: the assistant chief, who left his small-engine repair service unattended; Don, a butcher; Lane, a lean, wiry man who lives to ride bulls; and me. A few years back, Don donated a kidney to his niece. Inexplicably, he came out of surgery with one eye severely crossed. He jokes about it, calls himself the One-Eyed Beagle. He once butchered a mountain lion. Lane recently had the muscles of his right forearm stripped from the bone in a factory accident. His arm is splinted, his hand feels nothing.

We headed out into the country in three vehicles: a van, a pumper, and a tanker. We found the fire and put it out. Afterward, we joked with the assistant chief about how he got stuck on a command consisting of one firefighter with one eye, one firefighter with one arm, and one firefighter who was the first volunteer in village history to miss the monthly meeting because of a poetry reading.

Ours is a tiny town of 485 souls. Fluctuations in enrollment keep the school perpetually teetering on the brink of consolidation. Good jobs, when they are to be found, are often 30 or 40 miles away. During the day, the streets are still. It is from this shallow pool that the community must skim its firefighters, and I met the primary qualifications: I was frequently home during the day, and I had a pulse. Enrollment in volunteer fire companies is in nation-wide decline, and we are no different. If a call comes on a weekday, we are likely to have more fire trucks than firefighters to drive them. While we play host to an unprecedented migration of ur-banites fleeing the city in search of the "authentic" life, most of these new residents seem uninterested in lending a hand. They want peace and quaint, but they also want two-minute fire trucks to protect them on the cozy frontier. A few years ago I listened to a newly arrived back-to-the-lander rhapsodize about her own per-sonal Walden Pond. In the next breath, she described her shock at the 45-minute school bus ride her daughter was forced to endure. "I called the principal and told him that would have to change." Wait until Susie lights off the drapes and you need a fire truck, I thought.

I remember one of my first fire calls, in the heart of winter, after midnight, a woman's voice on the phone. Cabin fire. Way out in the tules, lakeside. When we got there it was an incandescent stack of Lincoln Logs. Two of us pulled an attack line and moved in. We tried to work together, but we were wading around in six inches of water over a bed of ice. Mostly, we looked like a pair of hockey goalies wrestling an anaconda. A lieutenant beckoned, pointing back over his shoulder. He turned to lead the way, I swung the hose, forgetting to shut it down first, and it got away from me. A torrent of water as thick as a blacksmith's forearm lifted the lieutenant's helmet and smacked him in the back of the neck. By the time we got back to town, it was dawn. At the lone convenience store, the locals were picking up coffee for the drive to work. I waited in line to sign for diesel, and one of them turned to look at me.

"Fire?" he asked. I was wearing sooty bunkers, a fire helmet, and my shirt was drenched.

"Yep," I answered.

"Where?"

"Out north a ways."

"Stop it?"

"From spreading."

We nearly made the millenium without 911. Until last month, whether for a grass fire or heart attack, you dialed a seven-digit number that rang in the homes of everyone on the department. Now we're summoned by pager, but some tradition survives: The old-timers still call the old number, and the first person to the fire hall still triggers the water-tower siren.

Among the firefighters who may show up are a pair of butchers, a trucker, a farmer, a carpenter, a mailman, and a mother of four. There are two sets of three brothers on the department. One of my younger brothers outranks me; it is frequently his duty to put me in harm's way. I shouldn't have teased him for not being able to draw when we were in grade school. Once, at a barn fire, deep inside the structure, I remember recognizing the two firefighters ahead of me as my brothers. We were arranged along the hose in order of birth, from youngest to oldest.

Because our department is small and the area we cover is far-flung, we joke that our proud motto is, "We've never lost a base-ment!" And in truth, while we make more "saves" than you might surmise, our most important task is usually to preserve as much of the structure as we can and protect everything surrounding it. Preservation enhances any subsequent investigation. And what is preserved may sometimes prove to be invaluable artifacts; after all, a house fire is a destruction of the past. There are people here losing their history.

Sometimes, when you're feeling reckless, you forget that. It's dangerous to get reckless, but it happens. There's an undeniable thrill in fighting fire. There are as many reasons to volunteer for this job as there are firefighters, but at some level most of us have a perverse hunger for danger, a desire to be tested, to survive — literally — a trial by fire. I feel this recklessness sometimes, but it never lasts long. *Fire Rescue Magazine* runs a column titled, "In the Line of Duty." It never lacks material. Article VI, Section 5, of our department's by-laws, a copy of which you are provided upon joining, outlines the procedure for draping the headquarters in mourning.

Of course, remove the danger and firefighting is just plain fun. You get full-grown toys, you get to drive fast, you get to spray water. Guys who join up for these reasons roar off to their first fire, and it's a rush, and they're all hot-damn and rock 'n' roll. Then the fire's out, and we spend three hours mopping up, and then another two hours back at the station scrubbing hoses and running checklists, and two or three calls later they just sort of fade away.

Many small-town volunteers feel an unclichéd sense of civic duty. I see it as an alternative to writing a check for some bureaucratic megacharity. We like the idea that when there is trouble, we're the ones sent in. But the whole "bold and brave" thing gets overblown. I receive a catalog every few months filled with everything from shoulder holsters to disposable handcuffs. It also features a range of popular novelty t-shirts for firefighters. *We walk where the Devil dances*, and *We go to hell so you don't have to*, and *I fight what you fear*. Ash buckets, say I. Self-aggrandizing claptrap. We study, we prepare, but the fact remains: We are amateurs playing a game in which the professionals regularly get their tails whipped. I fear what I fight.

I didn't grow up wanting to be a firefighter. I left town a farm boy, a good student, a fair defensive end. I returned twelve years later a long-haired writer with two hands so soft they might have belonged to a debutante. Shortly after the move back, I stopped by the monthly fire meeting. The chief motioned me into the fire garage. He is a stout man, burly but friendly. By day he dispatches freight trucks. "Try on these boots," he said. "We've got a helmet around here somewhere." Someone handed me a stiff pair of old fire pants — bunkers, they're called. A farmer in a bar jacket showed me how to shift the pumper, his cigarette a singalong dot dancing from word to word.

The local fire board does eventually require that you attend a firefighting course. Ours was laced with fascinating arcana. About ladders, for instance. We learned about aerial ladders, ground ladders, extension ladders, roof ladders, attic ladders, and pompier — or scaling — ladders. The bed and the fly. The basis for positioning a ladder fly-in or fly-out. Dogs and pawls, hooks and toggles. Rails and rungs. Truss blocks, tie rods, and tormentor poles. You'll find a set of angled spikes at the base of some ladders. They're called butt spurs. Sounds like *accoutrements* for a dominatrix, or some sort of localized arthritis. We learned not to simply yank a ladder off the truck and raise it any which way. For every foot of working height, the butt of the ladder should be four inches out from the wall. The fly should be raised at least three rungs above the roofline. A few years back, our local department decided to rehearse ladder placement at the Lutheran church. Fire officials forgot to warn the pastor. They'd gotten the trucks around and the ladders up when here he came, running down the middle of the street from the parsonage in his slippers, robe flapping, eyes wide.

The training exercises were a lark. We learned to unfurl a 50-foot roll of hose by underhanding it like a bowling ball. We raced a stopwatch to see who could gear up most quickly. We practiced spraying figure eights, the fat, three-inch hose stiff and insistent, shuddering with the power of pressurized water. Once, the largest student in class — well over six feet tall, 250-pound range — let his attention lapse at the nozzle. The hose tipped him over as easily as if he had been nudged by an elephant. We had a good laugh.

The instructor arranged an obstacle course. I waited my turn, swaddled from helmet to steel-toed boots in heavy turnout gear, sealed in the intimate, portable environment of the SCBA mask, that transparent barrier between toxic smoke and pink lungs, able to hear little beyond the easy huff and chuff of the respirator. I felt utterly isolated and protected, the way I'd felt as a child curled up in the darkness inside a cardboard box fort. We crawled around the course in pairs, the back partner clinging to the strap on the leader's air pack. Always partner up, never become separated, said the instructor. Gripping the strap, face-down, unable to see, I tried to raise my head. The oxygen hose resisted, prying the mask from my face, breaking the seal. A rush of air hissed out around my ears. I realigned the mask, and the hissing stopped. I still couldn't see. Scrabbling forward, I heard a clang. My oxygen tank had struck the underside of a fire truck, wedging me against the floor. I was suddenly air-hungry. The measured huff and chuff of the respirator became more insistent. Claustrophobia pressed in. Sweat leaped to my skin. The motion sensor attached to my collar began to caw. An image flashed: Flames. Heat. Dark smoke, thick as poison pudding. Pinned against the concrete, unable to see, unable to move, I suddenly understood what panic for oxygen might drive a man to do. I sucked air out of the tank faster and faster, wasting it, trying to keep up with my heartbeat. My partner wriggled free. I lost my grip on his strap. The low-air alarm sounded, an incongruous, flatulent ting-a-ling. A thought presented itself, unbidden: You can die doing this.

Nonetheless, fire is a tantalizing enemy. It has an undeniable pull. It lures you close, dares you inside. But as a firefighter, you must look beyond fire's hypnotic face. You see fire, you see it billow and snap, you watch it do its angry, amorphous dance, and you are mesmerized into believing it has no more shape than a soul. But to a firefighter, fire is fundamentally geometric. Five minutes into our first evening class, the instructor drew a triangle on the chalkboard. Then he labeled each point: heat, fuel, and oxygen. "The fire triangle," he announced. The fire triangle isn't fire; it is only the potential for fire. For fire made manifest, you need one more ingredient: An uninhibited chemical reaction. "The fire tetrahedron," said the instructor, replacing the triangle. He looked around the room. "Remove any one element of the tetrahedron, and you put out the fire." It's that simple.

Until you get there. The geometry of fire is one thing. The behavior of fire is another. It grows in volatile stages. First, the incipient phase, in which a fire is born. Rollover, in which combustible vapors accumulate at ceiling level, then explode into a rolling "fire front." The free-burning phase. Flashover, in which an entire room becomes superheated to the point of simultaneous ignition. The smoldering phase. And then, the Hollywood-friendly grandaddy of them all: *backdraft*. If a fire in a tightly sealed house cycles through the phases and depletes the available oxygen, it will settle into a brooding stasis. The house groans for air, and if you swing your axe through the door, you'll be blown across the yard like a flaming marshmallow out of a blast furnace. Should you awaken, you will likely do so in the nearest intensive care burn unit.

But you can't just focus on the fire. A house is burning. I am alone in a fire truck, dieseling through the darkness. The strobes sweep the swamp, skitter across the sawgrass. I hold the wide wheel, sort through the gears. In the small of my back, I can feel the willful momentum of 2300 gallons of shifting water — nine-and-a-half tons of mass in motion, ready to catch me goofing off, push me straight on a curve, drive me so far into the tag alders they'll have to fish me out with a rake. There was a pie chart in *Fire Chief* magazine this year, and a fat green slice of it floats in my head: 30.7 percent of firefighter deaths occur on the road to or from the fire. When it comes time to corner, I back off the accelerator, turn the wheel with both hands, hold my back straight as if I were balancing eggs on my head. As if the alignment of my spine could keep this truck from rolling over.

For all the cinematic potential—screaming sirens, roiling slugs of luminous, milky-orange smoke foaming the black night sky — most fire-fighting deaths have very little marquee value. The firefighter who dies spectacularly — silhouetted in a nimbus of flame with a child in his arms—is a reality, but a rarity. More likely, he'll be crushed under a falling wall. Get brained by a waterlogged beam. Fall through a floor. Touch a ladder to a power line. Run out of air in some hallway. Or have a plain, old-fashioned heart attack. Mostly, fire fighting is about anticlimax. The battle rarely ends in heroic conquest or deep tragedy. Oh, it's dangerous, all right, and not to be taken lightly, but what we're basically doing out there, when we haul our hoses out to crackling minivans and smoking garages, up smoldering silos, over sizzling rooftops, and down into basements, is trying to—as the old-timers say—put the wet stuff on the red stuff.

Springtime. A farmer calls. He's been planting corn near a swamp. His orange tractor has backfired, the sparks have lit last year's bleached canary grass. By the time I get there, the brush buggy is parked at the edge of the field. The lieutenant I drenched last winter is handing down backpack cans. I run around the front of the buggy and he hits me right between the eyes with a stream of water. "Know what that was for?" He's grinning wide. I grin back, shrug into the shoulder straps. And then we jog off toward the tree line, hauling our wet stuff toward the red stuff, a lumbering pair of deconstructionist geometricians looking to turn tetrahedrons into triangles. ◄

▶ Falling Together

An elderly woman has fallen in the street. It is London, noon, rush hour. She lands violently, on her buttocks and elbows, her head snapping back on impact. Her capacious white poke of a purse pinwheels across the zebra crossing, spitting handkerchiefs, pill bottles, a compact, pens, bits of paper, a trove of clutter. Thirty yards up the road, the traffic light switches to green, releasing a horde of small cars. The purse slides to a halt, bright and gaping in the sun, the white plastic brilliant against the oily tarmac. The cars surge forward, toward the old woman.

Seated in the upper level of a double decker bus stopped at a light, I'm looking down on traffic. The bus is enclosed, a sleek, soulless version of the classic red double-decker. A morning of un-relenting sun has turned it into a rolling hothouse. Several passengers are smoking; the smoke and the sun have worked behind my eyes, and the inklings of a headache have begun to seep through my temples. I'm tracking the cars and considering sleep when the flash of the white spinning purse catches my eye.

The woman next to me squawks and whips on point like a weathervane, her arm extended stiffly, index finger waggling. The old woman is just off the front of the bus and in the opposite lane. Her cheerfully patterned dress has flown above her waist, revealing doughy thighs and gray cotton underpants. But she has seen the cars, and her fear eclipses her mortification. Weeping and screaming, she claws at the sky, her fingers splayed and crooked, as if she hopes to hook the air and find her feet. The cars are gaining speed. She kicks a leg straight, and a shoe flips loose, arcing up and over her head, then skittering to the gutter. The heel is broken, set at an unnatural cant, like a dislocated thumb. On the bus, the passengers are on their feet. They gasp and ogle, bump shoulders for a clearer view.

An old man lurches from the curb, running to the woman with herky-jerky steps, as if he is on the strings of a palsied puppeteer. His loose brown pants flap at his shins. He bends stiffly, at the hips and knees, and reaches both hands to the woman. His eyes are wide, his fingers set to trembling so violently I can see them flutter from the bus. His jaw is working, his mouth springing open and closed as if he has a tongueful of hot food. The couple's hands meet and clasp, the old man tugs and shuffles backward. She is nearly upright when his grip fails, and she crashes back to the pavement.

I find myself rising from my seat, intent on disembarking. I will flag traffic. Pull the woman to safety. Put an arm around the old man's shoulders, lead him safely to the curb. The thoughts are reflex, and I am just off the cushions when the bus lumbers ahead and the woman is cut from view. On my feet now, I crane my neck with everyone else, and see only the pack of cars, their headlong charge unabated. Two blocks farther on, someone flags the toothy hospitality woman and orders tea in a paper cup. The sun is tropical. Ten minutes later, I doze.

Ten years later. I am passing through London and think of the old woman. I would like to think the cars stopped. Perhaps they didn't stop. Perhaps they did stop, but in the fall she broke a hip, and her husband came to the hospital room holding miniature daffodils cut from their garden. Perhaps she never went home again. Her story is part of my story, but in my story, her story ends without conclusion.

If you accept that time is linear, and that we are propelled by time, it follows that life is a proposal of position and momentum, and that we are continuously hurtling through an infinite bristle of convergence. Yesterday I folded cilantro into a venison stir fry using a spatula hewn from a tapered strip of birch. It was carved by an old man in Norway. We met briefly over a small dinner in his sister's garden. He spoke only Norwegian. Taking his leave, he simply handed me the spatula and smiled. I knew seven phonetically-memorized Norwegian words, and used three of them: "*Monge tusen takk* — many thousand thanks." A decade later, I bring out the spatula several times a week. I stir water chestnuts and thyme, and wonder if the old man still lives.

One need not leave the La-Z-Boy, much less ride a bus through London or hitchhike across Norway to transect a fragment of drama or intimacy. Like the actors in Luis Buñuel's *Phantom of Liberty*, we are simply Brownian particles made flesh, following a fractured arc defined as much by chaos as purpose. But when we wander, when we step outside the familiar, by choice or by chance, the reductive powers of displacement effect a distillation that casts distinct events in sharp relief. The old woman's tragedy becomes mythic; unable to reach her, I leave her forever in the street, forever before the onrushing traffic. The old man's spatula becomes totemic; passed from his hand to mine, it represents the intimate, fleeting points of intersection we find only on the wander.

Shedding the mundane everyday, and moving, always moving, the wanderer experiences a constant juxtaposition of intimacy and transience that produces a chronology of focal points to which we anchor distinct moments in time. An old woman falls and screams, and shows me the primal soul of her. An old man hands me a blade of wood and I cook with it forever. We share an intimacy far exceeding the intimacy I feel for people I see daily.

Sleeping under a small tent in the outskirts of Budapest just before the fall of communism, I was awakened after midnight by a thief kneeling on my feet. I remember the darkness, and the sound of his fingers rustling through my backpack, his breath as he leaned above me, and I remember the fear that flash-froze my guts. My first thought was of home. Then I rared up and drove my fist into his face. He rolled backward out the tent, and I heard his feet pound away in the dark. I wonder about the thief sometimes, who he might have been, what he might have intended, and how it is that we came to converge, as close as skin on skin, linked forever, even as we ricochet away at the speed of time. ◄

▶ What We Want

We can call him Al. It's the name he used in Belize City, and I wouldn't presume to improve upon it. Paunchy in his polo shirt, he appeared on the balcony of the Seaside Guest House and let himself into a tiny single room hardly larger than a public restroom stall. He was wearing acid-washed jeans and white tennies, and looked to be on the early edge of 50. The day previous, the guest house teemed with the usual motley lot of backpackers and daytrippers: a dreadlocked Austrian, a clean-scrubbed American Mormon, a Canadian fry cook from Florida, a pair of dusty, hippie-beautiful women from the Netherlands. Now they were all gone, off to catch a bus to Guatemala, or water taxis to the Cayes. Where they had all appeared worldly and roadworthy, Al I could picture back in the States, wearing slacks and a name tag, selling home appliances in a strip mall. The others looked like they'd traveled here. Al looked like he'd been caught here.

The Seaside Guest House is run by Quakers, and it is optimistically christened. You can *smell* the sea from the second floor, if the wind is right, and should the palm leaves part to provide a sight line over the tin roofs and down the adjacent alley, you might spy a scintilla of Caribbean glint, but knock your Belikin bottle over the balcony railing and you'll ding a taxi, not a sunbather. At the far end of the balcony, two doors form a right angle. One opens into the tiny single room Al entered. The other opens on a common room furnished with a few chairs and a simple table. A hallway leads from the common area to a handful of double rooms and at the far end, the bathroom. Just off the common area, at the head of the hall, is a bunk room crammed with six beds, one of which was mine. The bunk room and Al's room share a common wall.

Below the rooms, the first floor is taken up with a few tables, an abbreviated breakfast counter, and a small storage room. A young man named Omar mans the admissions desk. Behind Omar, in an office nook, the proprietor passes the time by reading. He is whip-thin, soft-spoken, and given to peering professorially over his half-glasses. I spoke with him the day Al arrived, and he said he taught part-time at the university. Throughout our brief conversation, he was methodically unsealing envelopes, his long fingers moving like deliberate, articulated caterpillars. The guest house is girded by a tall wooden fence and a locked gate that opens directly on Prince Street. Shortly after he entered his tiny room, Al re-emerged, descended the stairs, let himself out the gate, and disappeared down the street.

It was quiet after Al left. I sat at a table in the common area, composing notes toward a story on Belizian firefighters. When the hot breeze blew, the palms rattled like rain. Across Prince Street, a little old man, his face a wizened pecan, sat under an orange Ovaltine cap on a chair in the sun. Now and then he spoke to a woman ironing in the shade of the great white house that dominated the garden. The woman was built like an oil drum, wrapped in a vast white apron that bulged from her gut like a sail full of wind. Their soft Spanish floated across Prince Street and up through the screen.

A local reporter arrived and drove me to a seaside club, where we sat at an open-air table overlooking the water, eating chips and salsa spiked with cilantro and chunks of raw conch. At dusk, a squall kicked up and drove inland in a darkening smear. The wait staff moved around the deck, unfurling canvas curtains as the first rain spit through. I noticed a man standing alone at the railing, hands in his pockets, faced into the wind. It was Al. At his back, disco lights swabbed the barren dance floor. When the reporter and I left, the floor had drawn a few dancers. Al was on the fringe, hanging back.

Back in the guest house just after midnight, I have the six-bunk dorm room to myself. It's a cheapskate's special: the dorm room, at the dorm room rate, with no roommates — save for a beetle the size of Delaware that click-clacks across the floor when I switch the light on. I make a few notes in my journal, then settle in to sleep.

I waken some time later. Someone is fumbling with a door. Al has returned, and it sounds as if he has a friend. A woman is giggling. The wall between us is made of gapped one-inch boards; a few hairline strips of light seep through with the sound. I hear the bunk creak, hear the woman's voice. Switching between Spanish and Creole, she sounds pleasantly, lazily drunk, her voice a slurring purr. Al begins to petition her for specific favors. She giggles alcoholically, but remains firm on one point: *"Condom! Condom!"* He protests, quietly and urgently. She mentions a young daughter, asks for more tequila. I hear the bottle tip. I hear Al's voice again, and again, rather loudly this time, she insists that he produce a condom. He shushes her, but soon I hear the rattle of the wrapper. It becomes quiet. I hear weight shifting. Still no words. More sounds of movement. There is trouble. Al can't get hard. He makes another request. She demurs — "It will taste bitter." Again, he shushes her. The drinking and negotiations continue. Soon she is on a bipolar drunk, looping from coy to surly. At one of her low points, she mumbles about suicide. Then she brightens, asks for the bathroom. Al lets her in the main area, points her down the hall, then hides in his room while she pees noisily. Then I can see her reflection under my door. She is drifting around the common area. A chair creaks, and a newspaper crackles. It is quiet for a long time. Finally, Al stirs and creeps from his room. Then a harsh whisper: *"What the hell are you doing?!"* After much cajoling and shushing, he maneuvers her back to his room. But now she wants to leave. "This place is poison for me," she says. She asks if she can take the newspaper.

"Stay — I will make love to you in the morning," says Al.

"You will have to wake me up."

"I can go to your place," says Al, ever hopeful.

"My place is not so clean as this." She laughs bitterly.

"But I will be more relaxed there," says Al. The woman says nothing. Al speaks again. "Tomorrow I go to Caye Caulker. Meet me."

"Can I have cab fare?"

"No prob-lem-o." He shepherds her down the stairs and to the gate, shushing all the way. The gate clicks, and she is on her own. I hear him return to his room. I hear the condom wrapper crackle, hear him cap the tequila. Then he pads down the hall to the bathroom. My journal was on the floor beside my bunk. I've been taking notes in the dark. I press the light on my watch. It's 2:30 a.m. I'm a little guilty about the notes, but you find yourself privy to something like this, to the dialogue and circumstance of two people driven by two very different sorts of desperation, and you think you ought to turn it into some sort of parable. At the moment, I'm on my moral high horse, disgusted by a man who, unable to use her, would turn a woman loose in Belize City at this hour, leaving her to weave through the carnivorous back streets to her sleeping baby. But the story is more complex than that. It is about the human transactions we all make, about the hungers and incompletenesses that drive us, furtive and craven, into dark places, dark places that we inhabit only so that we may buy some time in the light. Worlds apart, separated by a lamina of social, cultural, and economic stratifications, Al and the woman were put on intersecting trajectories by twinned — not twin — needs. This is a damned lonely world, and given cover of darkness, we drive straight to the things we disdain by day. We want them hidden, but more than that, we want them.

Al is still in the bathroom when she returns. She is banging at the gate. "Al! Al! Al!" The mongrel dog who lies by the desk all day, soundless and unstirring, begins barking wildly. Now she is ringing the doorbell, again and again. Doors slam below. Omar and the manager are cursing the woman, yelling at her to leave. She calls out for Al. His reflection slides past my door as he returns from the bathroom. I can feel him holding his breath as he quietly lets himself out the main door and into his room, but she has spotted him.

"*AL! AL!*" The lock on his door clicks in place.

Now I hear the proprietor, no longer professorial. "It's that fucking guy in Room One!" His voice moves to the foot of the stairs. "You brought her in here, buddy, now make her leave! Tell her to go home!" Al's room is dark and silent. Downstairs, the yelling and door slamming continue. Omar cracks the gate and the woman wedges her foot in the jamb. Enraged, the proprietor grabs a machete and chases her down the street, into the darkness. For a while it is quiet. Then the proprietor's voice, from the foot of the stairs again.

"If you *want* a fucking whorehouse, *go* to a fucking whorehouse!"

And then it was quiet for good.

Al was gone in the morning. I caught a ride north, figured when I got back home, I'd write up the escapade as a humorous farce: "Likkered Up Hookers Ain't Nothin' But A Heartache," or some such. But it just didn't seem funny. I thought of him flying down here for hookers and snorkeling, and then I thought of me flying down here to fish for stories, a slumming voyeur armed with emergency traveler's checks and a plane ticket home, and I recognized that obscenity is relative. Scribbling away in my bunk, snuffling around the edge of this little story like a jackal just beyond the firelight, I was doing some skulking of my own. Given a front row seat at the disintegration of one man's fantasy, I found myself reviewing my own closeted collection of moldering ghouls and ossified indiscretions. If they were brought to light, would I live differently, or just more defiantly?

Our passions debase us. Our needs make fools of us all. ◄

▶ RSVP to the KKK

One morning in February of 1998, I found two pieces of mail in my mailbox. This essay is a reply to one of them.

Dear Grand Dragon Wayne:

Received your gracious invitation to participate in the White Pride Rally, Saturday, August 22, in Dyess, Arkansas. I am unable to attend. In lieu of my actual presence, please accept the following observations and recommendations, elicited by and culled from your flyer. Perhaps you can share my thoughts aloud at the end of the day when you gather 'round the flickering embers of the cross to toast marshmallows and let your hoods down.

First of all, your direct-mail technique is sterling. The hand-addressed envelope, the rubber-stamped return address, the letter-from-grandma size envelope, all work to create an "open me" feel. While the knight-on-a-rearing-horse icon is a bit fanciful, it is balanced nicely by the no-nonsense all-caps rendering of the National Association for the Advancement of White People acronym.

As to the flyer itself, I am quite taken with the hand-drawn border, festooned as it is with disembodied cartoony hoods — very Casper the Friendly Ghost. However, I note with perplexity that you have chosen to scratch out your typos — surely any self-respecting Grand Dragon would jump at the chance to use a little Wite-Out®. You might also wish to re-examine the photocopying process, as reproductive corruption of the caricatures of Grand Wizard Ray Larsen and Public Relations man Damon Lance Rose (That name — are you sure about this guy?) causes them to appear as morose, hooded black men being kissed on the brow by a bat-winged Easter chick.

I note with relief that *"THIS IS A FAMILY AFFAIR!"* with *"NO ALCOHOL, FIREARMS, DRUGS OR FIGHTING!"* and "WOMEN AND CHILDREN ARE MOST WELCOME." I don't need to tell you, Grand Dragon Wayne, or spell it out in underlined capital letters, that this country is going to heck in a handbasket, and I well note your dedication to the preservation of the extended family. It takes a village, y'know. It is also a testament to your perspicacity that in addition to food and beverages, you will be offering souvenirs. Good thinking. From Marxism to Lilith Fair, what's a movement without merch? Modern movements also require sponsors, and I see you've been so blessed by the National Knights of the Ku Klux Klan. Congrats. I am less enchanted by the fact that I will have the opportunity to "MEET POLITICAL SPEAKERS FROM AROUND THE COUNTRY." Can't we keep politics out of this? Hell, Grand Dragon Wayne, you know you can't trust politicians. You get them involved, and before long you'll have to take a senator to dinner, fill out thirteen forms, and complete a ten-year environmental impact study just to burn one little ol' cross. The upside? When it's time to take it to the streets, your politician friends may be able to expedite the parade permit process.

I am also in receipt of the NAAWP application form. While it turns out I'm not eligible (The breakdown: native-born — yes; loyal United States Citizen — yes, by and large; white — seems like it, but I've not done my genealogy homework, and I tan with suspicious speed and depth; temperate habits — yes, at least the ones I admit to; of Christian faith — not to your satisfaction; and, believe in White Rights and Americanism — see Christian faith), I'm intrigued by the box that says "I am a former member and would like to be reinstated." I assume this is in compliance with your Christian faith prerequisite (forgiveness, the prodigal son, etc.,) but I wonder: Will dues be pro-rated?

Okay, Grand Dragon Wayne, joke's over. Here's the deal. I don't curse much, but when I opened your letter in our little post office, the temperature in my gut dropped twenty degrees and I said something very nasty indeed. Your sentiments slithered right into my tiny home town, right into my mailbox, right into my hand. That disturbs me. Did you think I was some sort of Aryan rough boy? From the way you addressed my letter I can tell you got my name from a series of articles I wrote for a working-class magazine. One on a country music star and his gun store. One on snowmobile racing. And one on monster trucks. Apparently I fit your recruitment profile. You must have missed my piece on the contributions of black artists to country music.

Well, Grand Dragon, it's true that no one will mistake me for an Ivy League-educated liberal professor of multicultural studies any time soon. I hunt. I own guns. I own my share of camouflage clothing. I'm a loner. I shave infrequently. My transport of choice is a beat-up pickup truck. I've been known to sing old country music songs at the top of my lungs with no trace of irony. I know my way around the woods at night, and harbor a touch of disdain for anyone who doesn't. But don't save me a beer at the rally.

I despise you, but in a more complex way than you might suspect.

I despise you not just because you are a racist, but because you obscure the true complexities of racism and serve as an easy out for anyone seeking superficial absolution. You are frightening, Grand Dragon Wayne, and you are dangerous, but you are out in the open. In a country hung up on skin, you are the equivalent of a wart — unattractive, perhaps even pre-cancerous, but easily identifiable, and, if need be, easily removed.

Meanwhile, the real problems facing us are much more in the character of a metastatic melanoma — a deadly malignancy with tendrils that lace the entire substructure of society. Your type serves as a lightning rod to divert our focus from the deeply insidious nature of prejudice and racism. We get you on *Jerry Springer*, make fun of your hood, shout you down, engage in group behavior the equivalent of poking a dumb animal with a stick, and then, having solved nothing, hit the remote feeling a self-congratulatory shot of vindication. Meanwhile, you head home too much the true believer to be humiliated, and likely having made a convert or two. Thinking we know who's to fear and who's to blame, we stop questioning. If racism were woven with a thread as pure as your white sheet, stripping it out would be a simple matter indeed. Unfortunately it is woven in all shades. In fine, delicate strands. And it is interracial as hell. It is as blatant as spray-painted epithets and as subtle as an averted gaze. It storms through the streets, but even more frequently it coasts through the suburbs in a minivan. It thwarts human endeavor, it plays both ways, it is used as leverage, it is roundly ignored. Its greatest toll is exacted not through white-hot hate, but through distrust and sadness.

I also despise you because you remind me that we live in a world where bumper stickers pass for intelligent discourse, Grand Dragon Wayne. You've seen them: "You Can't Hug Your Children With Nuclear Arms." "When Guns Are Outlawed, Only Outlaws Will Have Guns." "Think Globally, Act Locally." "Mean People Suck." "I'm [insert indignant term here] and I Vote." Etc., and yaddety. None of these one-dimensional aphorisms stand up well under examination, and I remain suspicious of anyone who can express their most deeply-held convictions in the space of a bumper sticker. But that's the way we've come to deal with things. Pick out the obvious, yell at or about it, and click off the remote feeling self-righteous. No heavy lifting required.

Simply railing at you is like displaying a bumper sticker — it makes me feel better, looks good to my assumed constituency, but accomplishes little in the big picture. There is enough disingenuous behavior on both sides of the race issue to suggest that the true path to reconciliation can only happen on a personal level, one-to-one. So I'm taking this personally, Grand Dragon Wayne. You and me. I hope to undermine you by taking your invitation, making fun of it in public, and then, more importantly, pointing out that as nasty as you are, you are only a marginal, distracting symptom of a systemic problem.

A guy like me, Wayne, I pay the rent by writing, a little piece about monster trucks here, and essay about the joys of summer there, all the while hoping I'll have a chance to write something of greater importance some day. You've given me that chance, and I'm taking it. But I don't mind telling you the fact that you know where I live frightens me. The fact that you sat down with a pen and wrote my name and hometown on an envelope makes me want to stay away from windows.

Do y'like irony, Grand Dragon Wayne? Hope so, because then you'll love this: When I found that envelope in my mailbox, it was nestled cheek-to-cheek with a letter from the Southern Poverty Law Center. They were asking me to support their "Teaching Tolerance" program. To take their "Tolerance Challenge," and "say 'yes' to tolerance." I admit I'm reminded of the bumper stickers. And their envelope was a mass-mailing job; no handwritten address. They probably don't even know where I live. But I think I'll send'em a little something. Your name and address, for one thing.

Have a nice summer. ◀

► Fear This

My fear is my substance, and probably the best part of me.
                                                —*Franz Kafka*

I don't get to town much, so being cut off in traffic should have been a novelty. A stream of bumper-to-bumper day-jobbers dron- ing homeward, doing sixty in a forty-five, light turning red 200 yards ahead, and this non-signaling knothead shoots in front of me like he's going for the pole at Daytona. Pinches himself be- tween me and some four-door, and then stomps the brakes like he's smashing a rat. And so I sat behind him, wondering if I had time to rip out his valve stems before the light changed. His base- ball cap was on backward, of course, his stereo — as I am confi- dent he would have put it — was "cranked," and he was driving one of those yappy little four-wheel drive pickups that have be- come the toy poodles of the truck world. But while all of these things triggered my pique, it was the "No Fear" sticker in his rear window that sustains my rant.

The "No Fear" logo represents a line of clothing and sports gear. Irksomely ubiquitous on windshields, t-shirts, caps, billboards and bumper stickers, this bellicose bit of marketing has caused me to ponder what I know of fear. Very little, I suspect. Not be- cause I am immune, or brave, or drive a hot little truck, but be- cause of good fortune, and because what fear I have experienced — in the face of a well-armed Hungarian border guard, in the back of a fire engine, down a Belize City back street — has been, in the scope of things, fairly superficial. But in today's society, where re- bellion amounts to a nipple ring, a Kool-Aid rinse, or an exquisite tattoo, superficial covers it. Image — be it ephemeral as a cathode ray and thin as ink on a two-syllable bumper sticker — while it is so obviously nothing, is, in the age of identity purchased at retail, everything indeed. And every marketer believes — that is not to say they understand — the words of French playwright Jean Anouilh: "An ugly sight, a man who is afraid." Fear is ugly, and ugly doesn't sell sunglasses.

But what sort of vacuous buffoonery allows us to adopt such slogans? Consider the case of the lump of gristle with a pulse who cut me off in traffic. Cossetted in a society where rebellion has been co-opted by commerce, where individuality is glorified in fashion campaigns that put youth in worldwide lockstep with an efficiency despots only dream of (assuming, of course, that the people who own athletic shoe companies are not despots), raging youth finds itself sitting at a red light, steeped in the same hormonal invincibility that fuels ravaging armies, with nothing to do but wait to tromp the accelerator of a trendy little pickup. Who knows fear?

I once hitchhiked a ride with a Belizian cane hauler. I couldn't speak Spanish; he couldn't speak English. It didn't matter: the bellowing engine precluded conversation. We simply grinned at each other as he hurled the truck through the twists in the road, the scorched sugar cane swaying high above our heads. The truck was of indeterminate vintage. The play in the steering was such that an entire half-spin of the wheel was required before the truck's vector was affected. The previous evening, on a blind corner, a pickup had veered over the center line, crashing head-on with a tractor hauling cane. Two men had been killed. As we shot the same curve that morning, the wreckage still remained; grieving clusters of family stood along the roadside. We hit that curve full tilt, blowing a backwash of cane leaves over the upended tractor. I sneaked a peek at the speedometer. It was completely obscured by a circular decal of the Virgin Mary. We grinned at each other again.

Two men, both driving dangerously in trucks, both expressing themselves through adhesive symbology. And yet there is a difference; an instructive distinction.

Is the cane hauler wiser because he knows fear? Poverty, dangerous labor, the hungry faces of a brood at home — surely these cultivate acquaintance with fear. The Virgin Mary decal seems evidence of theistic fear. But these are presumptive conclusions, and, I think, just miss the point. That point being, if the cane hauler drives without fear it is because he has acknowledged fear, and then turned it over to the Blessed Virgin. The fellow in the four-wheel poodle, on the other hand, is fearless because he has never been forced through circumstance to acknowledge fear's existence. He has made the quintessentially American mistake of thinking his life is special, his bumper sticker is bold, his truck is shiny . . . because *he* is special. His fearlessness is an inane statement construed through an accident of birth. In contrast, the cane hauler may dispense with fear, but he knows better than to scoff it.

Ernest Hemingway wrote about people living "essential, dangerous lives." Those three words say so much about what we are or aren't, and explain why, in a world filled with fear, we would choose to disguise the sheltered nature of our existence through mindless sloganizing. Perhaps the pickup driver could back up his bravado; swagger through a Rwandan refugee camp, exhort those pitiful laggards to get a set of decent basketball shoes, hoist a microbrew, and shake off this unattractive predilection to fear. Tell'em this is Planet Reebok, and on Planet Reebok, we have no room for the fearful. Better yet, he could earn his "No Fear" decal by strapping on his favorite Nikes and sprinting down Sniper Alley beside a 12-year-old Sarajevan on a water run.

Somehow, after that, I think he'd prefer to keep his rear window clear, the better to see what fearful thing might be creeping up on him. ◄

▶ The Haul Road

Notes for non-truckers: Western Star is the brand name of a Canadian-made semi tractor. The average fully-loaded semi running on a smooth concrete highway "grosses" roughly 80,000 pounds. The term "90-weight" refers to an extremely high viscosity engine oil. The "fifth wheel" is a large steel plate that serves as the point of attachment between the semi tractor and trailer. A "Jake" is a specialized braking device that allows a trucker to throw a switch and essentially make the engine work against itself.

If you stick your rig in the ditch along Alaska's treacherous Haul Road, the word starts traveling before the white leaves your knuckles. For the next two weeks, every trucker you meet is a wise guy. You may stop for a bowl of bean soup at Coldfoot and find a Polaroid of your wayward load tacked to the bulletin board. If the R-rated, irregularly published *Chuck Hole Gazzett* is up and running, you can expect your bad day to be immortalized in headlines like "Abe Omar Plows Snow," or, "A Shooting [Western] Star." But nobody laughs too hard or too long. Because up here, they have a saying about drivers who exit the Haul Road unexpectedly: "There are two types of truckers: Those of you who have, and those of you who will."

Tom McAlpine won't talk about whether he has or hasn't. "That's voodoo," he grins, and changes the subject. McAlpine has been making the run between Fairbanks and the oil fields of Prudhoe Bay since 1978, with a three-year break beginning in 1986, when the oil business tanked. He headed for the lower 48, where he worked on a ranch and ran produce. He refers to it as time he spent "outside." When the oil field action picked up again, he returned to Fairbanks, and he's been running the Haul Road ever since. Officially known as the Dalton Highway, the Haul Road was completed in 1974. It runs alongside the Trans-Alaska Pipeline, terminating at the Arctic Ocean. Its primary purpose is to supply drilling operations in the gigantic Prudhoe Bay oil field, 250 miles north of the Arctic Circle.

The map may say "highway," but down where the rubber meets the road, the Dalton is a skinny 400-mile scar of chuckholes, dust, mud, snowpack and black ice that winds its way up and down through swaths of forbidding pine forests, ragged-edge mountain passes and endless sweeps of tundra.

The head of the Dalton is around 85 miles from Fairbanks — the only stretch of what could reasonably be called "highway" on our route. We pulled out of Fairbanks at 10:30 a.m., grossing 101,400, our four-axle trailer loaded with 9,426 gallons of methanol, used in the oil fields to keep drill holes from freezing. Almost as soon as we got started, we pulled off the road to fuel the trucks and ourselves at the Hilltop truckstop, the last full-time services for 500 miles. The truck gorged on diesel, and we gorged on hot biscuits slathered in 90-weight gravy, served with fried potatoes on a plate half the size of a fifth wheel. Then we struck out.

As Tom McAlpine puts it, the first 130 miles of the Haul Road are "nothin' but shiftin'." We took many of the hills at 15 miles per hour, and McAlpine kept up a running commentary: "This one here has caught its fair share of trucks . . . See there where all those trees are flattened? Buddy of mine went in there a few weeks ago . . . This one's called Five Mile Hill . . . I stopped to dig a guy out of a car on this one. . . ." The litany continues: Gobbler's Knob. ("Misjudge that one, and you learn to back with your brakes locked!") Oil Spill Hill. The Roller Coaster. Sand Hill. ("This one will eat your lunch.") The Beaver Slide. ("Guy lost it here once, jammed it in a low gear and wound the engine up — there were wrist pins and connecting rods all over the road.")

For mile after rough mile, the big 600hp Cat in McAlpine's '99 Western Star 4964FX is either chomping up a grade or riding the Jake. We stop atop Two-and-a-Half-Mile Hill and walk around the truck, performing a visual inspection. Up here, the pines are daubed with fat licks of snow, and packed snow has taken much of the roughness from the road. "In the summertime, you stop here to count your tires, see how many you have left," jokes McAlpine.

The nature of the Prudhoe Bay run imposes itself on the trucks and truckers in many ways. McAlpine has to replace the peg on his CB mike with a steel bolt. "The bracket vibrates so much, it saws right through the plastic one," he says. Tires are run at low pressure to extend their life — still, they last only about 30,000 miles. Once started, engines are rarely shut down; all that idle time adds up to a 3.3 mpg lifetime average. Twin spotlights in the mirror racks are aimed at both ditches to illuminate moose — they like to run the Haul Road when they get tired of fighting deep snow. The intense cold can freeze axles in an instant; McAlpine always puts his truck in motion with a gentle left-to-right swerve, checking in the mirrors to see that all the flourescent orange stripes painted on his trailer wheels are spinning.

Sometimes it's not cold enough. "Zero to ten degrees, that's pretty good truckin'," said McAlpine as we left Fairbanks. But later that night, when we inched up Atigun Pass and over the Brooks Range, the Western Star's exterior thermometer read 33 degrees — just the right temperature to turn the snow pack into a water slide.

McAlpine drove on the edge of his seat. We had stopped to chain up before the climb — "Chains decrease the pucker factor," says McAlpine — but it was still a tense ride, waiting for the wheels to slip like someone waiting for a balloon to pop. Tom kept looking in the mirror to check his tires. Tires that run white are getting a good grip on the snow pack. Tires that run black are too warm —

they're melting, not gripping the snow. Our tires were running black, so Tom kept one eye out for traction-giving loose gravel at the edge of the road; at the same time, he has learned to distrust that edge — a sharp shoulder might be nothing more than graded snow.

Any trucker who has run a variety of weather and terrain will tell you the jokers in the Haul Road deck aren't unique. What is unique is how often those jokers come up. For 500 miles, the road demands constant attention. There's a gremlin waiting every quarter mile: an icy switchback, a love-crazed caribou, a whiteout, a chuckhole blowout that hangs your snout out over some godforsaken ravine.

One of the old hands, a man who goes by the handle of "Pappy," puts up white steel crosses where anyone has died. It's hardly the "tombstone every mile" that truckin' singer Cowboy Dick Curless sang about, but there are just enough of Pappy's crosses along the way to help you think about family waiting at home and grip that wheel a little more tightly.

Truckers meeting atop narrow Haul Road hills have been known to clip mirrors, but such incidents incite more ribbing than road rage. Out here, a sort of rough-hewn courtesy prevails. Each time we met an oncoming truck, each driver slowed, reducing the amount of gravel in the air. McAlpine's windshield is filled with cracks and stars, almost all of them put there by four-wheelers who don't know the rules (the Dalton Highway was only recently opened to the public).

When a pickup full of oilfield workers catches us crawling up the 9 percent grade of the Beaver Slide, they wait until we're about to crest, and then radio us. "Yeah, can we get around ya there?" McAlpine gives them the all clear. "Thank ya!" they radio as they zip past. The same thing happens when we're caught by a reefer running produce. The pass is arranged before it's executed.

Every time we meet a truck, McAlpine greets the driver by

name. They update each other on road conditions ahead and behind, maybe rib each other a little, but there's very little yakkety-
yakkety. "Down there on the 'outside' the CB is a toy," says
McAlpine, "but up here it's a necessity." He likes the fact that he
knows everyone on the road, likes knowing that if he gets in a jam,
the next truck through will pull over to help. "The old rules still
apply up here," he says.

It was long dark when we hit Coldfoot, the unofficial halfway
point of the Prudhoe run. Coldfoot is a lonely little outpost with a
restaurant that, depending on staffing, is sometimes self-service.
Midway through our bean soup, we were joined by Tom's father,
Del. He was running cement and had been playing catch-up all
day. He would make the rest of the run with us.

It was a Monday night; on our way out the door, we walked
past a handful of truckers watching TV. Many time zones away,
the Dallas Cowboys were spanking the Philadelphia Eagles, 34-0.
The twin Western Stars were idling in the lot. "Dad doesn't like to
have anyone out front of him," laughed Tom, and right on cue, Del
poured the cobs to 'er. The big blue cab torqued and bounced, and
off he went, his moose spotters punching twin holes through the
night.

In general, the Dalton Highway passes through three kinds of
terrain; aspen and pine-covered foothills on the Fairbanks end,
expanses of tundra on the Prudhoe end, and in between, the grand,
upheaved bulk of the Brooks Range. The stark breadth of the land
is stunning. "Sometimes out here," says McAlpine, "it's like somebody shut all the lights off, turned the heat down, and went home."

But the desolation is trumped by beauty. "Look at this," he
breathes in a voice as awed as a first-timer. We're in the Brooks
Range now, running with a view to the valley ahead. The moon is
fat and incandescent, cradled between two bleached peaks like a
bright bead in a gunsight. Ahead of us, and to both sides, every-

thing glows an electric white. "Sometimes," he says, "it looks like a giant black-light poster."

We heave and lurch through the moonlight, the mountains beginning to flatten into rolling tundra. The Western Star's 306" wheelbase takes some of the jolt from the road, which is actually much smoother now that we've reached the point where water trucks have been running, covering pits and ruts with a smooth layer of ice. Occasionally, an ice chunk or a rock will deliver a ringing shot to the frame.

By the time we hit the oil fields, it's 1:30 a.m. and I'm nodding off. Everything is socked in fog. Drilling superstructures, studded with halogen beacons, loom through the haze. Over the CB, we bid goodnight to Del, who will be unloading at another site. Then we park. As soon as the truck stops, Tom hauls a spill pad from his toolbox and puts it beneath his oil pan — environmental regulations forbid even the tiniest drip of oil on the snow. Then he pokes his head into a portable office and checks the unloading schedule. He's in line to be unloaded and on his way home well before noon. He climbs in his bunk, and I sling my bedroll on the sleeper floor. And then, snug in my sleeping bag, I let that big Cat engine purr me off to the best night's sleep I've had in months.

There are times, out on the tundra, when the mercury slides to 40 or 50 below and the wind pushes the flexible delineators flat and puts up a horizontal wall of snow, that McAlpine pulls the rig over and idles for three days. He huddles in his warm little cube of air, eating MREs and waiting for the storm to pass. And there are times — when he's babying a trailer full of methanol up one side of the Brooks Range, wishing he had chained up and waiting for the tires to slip — that the fan on his Cat 600 kicks in, and he flinches like someone set off a cherry bomb in his sleeper.

And then there are those times, on the homeward end of a run, when he rounds yet another curve shouldering out over the pine tops and he sees one of Pappy's white crosses, that he's reminded that you don't run this road; it runs you.

But it's not all bad. As we left Prudhoe Bay the next morning, we saw two signs. One said we had 494 axle-busting miles to go; the other said, "DON'T BE GRUMPY." And for all the nasty surprises the Haul Road can spring, Tom McAlpine knows his run holds at least one attraction every trucker dreams of: "Once you get up here," he says, "you've got to go home. It's the end of the road." ◄

▶ The Road Gang

The road, at night. Thirty miles up in the rare cold black, the ionosphere bounces madness back upon the earth. Waves of amplitude modulation yo-yo from the sky, hopscotching squares of latitude and longitude. Roll the AM tuner and the dial winds through a netherworld; a pulsing, electrostatic ebb and swell of fuzz and flash. The ephemeral spirits in the machine spout prophecy and damnation, provide news without context, dawdle through the late innings of a White Sox game. Dante trips out with Marconi, and their nocturnal spawn dance the dash, dive through your head, chase you down no matter which way you travel.

The phrase "nocturnal spawn" would likely put Dave Nemo off his biscuits. He's an unassuming man, with a light, friendly tone. Put himself through college in New Orleans, on the barges and in the bars, pulling tow and playing country music. Got a part time job at WWL in New Orleans, but it was 1969, his lottery number was 17, and Uncle Sam was still taking. Wound up in Korea, on the overnight with Armed Forces radio. A year and a half passed, and he was back at WWL, broadcasting country music for truckers on a new all-night radio show they were calling The Road Gang. Twenty-five years later, he's still sending out skip, now from a tiny bunker of a studio a rock-toss from the Country Music Hall of Fame in Nashville. And the members of the Hall would approve. In the gold-plated era of radio consultants and computerized playlists, Nemo works with a box of recipe cards and has gone toe-to-toe with guys in ties. Radio is no business for a purist, and yes, Shania Twain commands a card. But the bulk of the names penciled in the mix run to the likes of Cash and Cline, Haggard and Jones, Williams and Wynette. You can still hear Lacy J. Dalton on the

Road Gang, or a teen-aged Tanya Tucker, or Tommy Collins — the man Merle Haggard called Leonard. Dale Watson is big with the truckers, and up until they caught the wave, BR5-49 used to drop by and pick a few on their way home from Robert's Western Wear. If you drive all night, you'll hear a pair of 15-minute Road Gang Hammer Down Bluegrass Breakdowns. Nemo keeps a banjo under his bed; sometimes he grins and says if he had his way, the Road Gang would be all-bluegrass, all the time.

The legendary American trucker isn't the hero he used to be. Clueless renegades, bad press and an ignorant public have all taken some of the shine from the stacks. Automakers love to tout their airbags and V-6 snap in the looming shadow of Tyrannosauric trucks. A van slides into the oncoming lane, and the *St. Louis Post-Dispatch* reads, "5 Killed As Tractor-Trailer Hits Van." Some yobbo in a bitsy four-wheeler sees a ten-foot patch of concrete off the front bumper of a Kenworth and homesteads it in a heartbeat. And last week's behemoth Mid-America Truck Show in Louisville was salted with the occasional log-book-bending *Deliverance* extra. But the bottom line is this: Taken as a whole, the best drivers on the road — men and women — are still truckers. Shut'em down, and the negative buzz will be obliterated by pampered howls of deprivation. On the Road Gang, truckin' songs are received without irony.

You'll hear truckers on the show. They are their own sort of skip, their lo-fi voices ranging the Rand McNally plat. Night Train is on the line. He has his landing gear down, and will sleep at home tonight. Bowlegged Snake checks in. Half Breed, T-Trucker, Six Pack, King Korn, Gatekeeper, they all make contact. Cherokee is in Fort Smith, headed to Pennsylvania. The Denver Dreamer is rolling through Denver. Jeff, no handle, no truck, isn't going anywhere — he's calling from an oil platform in the Gulf of Mexico.

The writing life took me to the Mid-America show last week. It was a good gig. Met the guys who haul the Budweiser Clydesdales. Helped Reba McEntire's truckers load out 12 semi trucks' worth of stage, rigging, and electrical tinsel. Took three days and sifted through about 25 acres of trucks and all things big rig. Come Saturday afternoon, I pulled out for home. Glanced at the map, slipped inside the blue vein of I-65, and rolled north out of Louisville. By the time I hit the Wisconsin line, I still had three hours to go. I kept the Road Gang tuned, punching between WWL and WLAC. Kevin Gaskin, Ol' Spiderbite, was covering for Nemo. He wished it was warmer, so he could go catfishing. Fugitive called from Albuquerque to talk about Hale-Bopp and remind everyone to watch for the eclipse. Pinkard & Bowden filled the "Trucker's Chuckle" slot. In NASCAR news, as always, the names were the same, but they said Earnhardt was struggling. Chaplain Joe Hunter checked in with Truck Stop Ministries to help Mr. and Mrs. Trucker down Heaven's Road. And between it all, the music: Johnny Paycheck. Jerry Reed. Roger Miller. Joe Stampley sang "She's Long-Legged," with a straight face. I was just home when Ol' Spiderbite pulled a new one from the recipe cards, something by a guy named Jack Ingram.

There are other trucking radio shows. The Trucking Bozo, out of WLW in Louisiana; Marcia Campbell and Jerry Minshall, with Interstate Radio Network. Bill Mack has been on the air for years. Wrote "Blue" for Patsy Cline; a girl named LeAnn Rimes recorded it a while later. But I heard Dave Nemo first, at 2 a.m., somewhere in the middle of North Dakota. And so, out of loyalty, when I'm on the road for the overnight, I drive as if my barnacled 1989 Tempo has 10 forward gears and a Georgia overdrive, usher in the skip, and collect my mile markers with the Road Gang. ◄

► Convoy

If you accept the hypothesis posited via airbrush on the cab of a giant purple Freightliner idling behind a Nebraska truckstop, the American economy lives and dies on 18 wheels: *Without Trucks, America Stops*. Evidence supporting the hypothesis? Virtually everything you purchased last year — whether you sat on it, wore it, listened to it, or ate it — was delivered by one of America's 3.1 million truckers. Trains, pipelines, and ships move more bulk commodities, but in 1996, 60 percent of all domestic freight — 6.5 billion tons — traveled by truck. Consequently, as the economy booms, so booms trucking. As of 1998, roughly 423,000 trucking companies were desperately competing for drivers at a rate projected to add between 40,000 to 80,000 new truckers to the road every year until 2005. A January 1997 *Time* magazine article ranked truck driving fifth on a list of the 15 hottest fields.

But who wants to be a trucker? The associations are rarely flattering. The leering sleazeball in *Thelma and Louise*. The cold-eyed gear-jamming kidnapper in *Breakdown*. A goofy Sylvester Stallone, arm-wrestling and dieseling a path to his son's heart in *Over The Top*. The Subaru Forester ad in the back of *Harper's*, with its beastly semi veering across the double yellow on a narrow mountain road (the family survives thanks only to the Forester's zippy, evasive all-wheel-drive system). The theme is repeated in any number of television commercials and reinforced on the news: trucks run the road like rhinos on a jailbreak, usually with a spectacularly distorted passenger vehicle on their snout. And it doesn't help when some 18-wheeler looms over your trunk, filling your mirror with a palette of dried bug guts pasted across a steel bumper the size of a chromed morgue slab. Suddenly you are Dennis Weaver in Spielberg's *Duel*, strung on a thin wire between terror and defiance. You hold your own, because by God this is your road, too, but what a confidence builder it must be to sit eight feet above the concrete, backed by 80,000 pounds of Big Mo. You look in the mirror again. I wonder, you think, what it's like up there.

And so you hitch a ride with a trucker.

The trouble with hitching a ride with a trucker is the lawyers. A truck wreck involving an unauthorized passenger is a litigation lollapalooza, and so most trucking companies have a no-riders policy. I knew this when I showed up with a backpack and a notebook at the Trucker's Jamboree in Waupun, Wisconsin, looking to hitch a ride on the Share America Convoy to Reno, Nevada. By the time I got to Dave Sweetman, I was batting oh-fer and expected to be turned down again. If you can't risk the liability, I said, I'll understand. He looked me over, then stuck a thumb over his shoulder. "See that?" I sighted along his thumb to the lettering on the side of his big green Kenworth. *Owned and Operated by David L. Sweetman, 3 Million Safe Miles.* He looked me square in the eye. "I reckon I can make it three million, two thousand."

And so, we put our tin in the wind.

It's interesting what you feel up there in the prow of that big ship. Powerful, certainly, what with those 475 horses chooglin' along at your feet, the turbo holding its high, thin note, sucking down air, turning it into miles, and blowing them out the twin stacks while the rest of the world sits still and falls behind. But you also feel a little tentative, a little out of control at the front end of all that length and momentum, like a flood victim sweeping downstream astride a duplex. And from up here, the cars — all of them, even the overblown SUVs — look flighty and irresponsible. They take on the nature of pests, and when they dart too close, or linger too long in the vast blind spots, you want to chastise them, tell them to get clear for their own sake. They are like little piglets who fail to realize that while mommy may wish them no ill, they must give her room to operate or risk being crushed.

As an owner-operator, Dave Sweetman owns his truck and leases his services to a car hauling company. Owner-operators are essentially self-employed. They enjoy more independence than company drivers, but they also have to keep a closer eye on the bottom line. Few are as established as Sweetman, and his truck, with all its *accoutrements* (including a stand-up shower), is not typical. Most truckers run with one eye on the road and one on the end of the month.

Sweetman's business card reads, *Transporter Of New Rolls-Royce, Bentley, Ferrari, Lotus, Antique and Classic Cars, Trucks, Boats, Airplanes, Movie, TV and Celebrity Cars Door To Door*. He's hauled the Batmobile and the Fred Flinstone car. He's delivered cars to Puff Daddy, Lenny Kravitz, model Tyson Beckford, and spent quality time tooling around with Jay Leno. The priciest car he ever hauled was a 1907 Rolls-Royce Silver Ghost, otherwise known as "The World's Most Valuable Automobile." When Sweetman eased it into his trailer, it was insured for $40 million. It takes a confident man to handle that kind of cargo, and Sweetman is a bit of a showboat. At Waupun, his tricked-out truck won a rack of trophies for which he feigned apathy. He says things like "absol-tute-ly." He speed-dials his dispatcher on a voice-activated cell phone by barking, "Butthead!" When he misspeaks, he lets loose a sharp tooth-whistle, as if he's summoning his runaway tongue, and cracks, "Brain-fade!" He's not cocky, but he operates with a contained swagger. Then again, he has navigated 79 feet worth of Kenworth over enough miles to circle the earth 140 times — through 25 years of every imaginable form of ugly weather and ugly traffic, with nary a fender-bender — all the while toting cargo valuable enough to finance a series of Whitewater investigations in perpetuity. There's a reason they've trusted him with the Silver Ghost six times in six years.

It's tough to recast the stereotypical trucker when he's all over the road. You don't remember all those trucks that run a polite line; you remember the one that squeezes you on a curve, the one that roars up and breathes down your neck, the one with the window sticker that reads, "Diesel Fumes Make Me Horny." An hour at a truckstop will only reinforce the worst caricatures. Recurring themes: bellies, cigarettes, and scruffy disgruntlement, often clad in overdue laundry. These are impressions not easily overcome. You have to stand right up and acknowledge them, for starters, which means we must put Dave Sweetman on cruise for a minute and talk about Share America Convoy organizer Gary King. He knows what you think of truckers, and he knows why.

"All our warts, wrinkles and bumps are out in the open," he says. "Whatever we do is pretty much observed." King is a former state trooper and Greyhound bus driver. Left all that to drive truck for 26 years. Too many years behind the wheel, too many Camel cigarettes, and too much truckstop food have saddled him with short breath and swollen feet. He's a big man. "I'm 260 pounds, used to be 300. I can be as mean and nasty as anybody." But he smiles when he says that, because he has seen what mean and nasty have done to trucking. "The trucking industry was always known for having a brotherhood, and that's fallen by the wayside," he says. "There comes a time when you have to say enough is enough." What he really wants is for us all to get along, to buddy up and share the road. And so a few years ago, he started Trucker Buddy International, a pen-pal program linking drivers with grade-school students. The truckers send letters and photos and souvenirs from the road, and drop by with their trucks now and then, and the kids learn about geography, and math, and commerce, and time, and distance. The kids would probably go bonkers if Shaquille O'Neal stopped by to play role model, but underperforming superstars are tough to book. Instead they get to meet a trucker who speaks with enthusiasm about a fundamental profession with no cheering section, and, as Dave Sweetman will tell me later, find out where potatoes come from. "Drivers have very few opportunities to give something back to society," says King, "even though they do it every day just by doing their job. This industry is the industry all others rely on." He hopes the convoy will help recruit drivers for the Trucker Buddy program, but he also hopes it will do a little something to rehab the image of the American trucker.

Trucking was born at the end of the 19th century, when gasoline engines began to replace horses. In 1912, a Packard truck delivered three tons of freight from New York City to San Francisco — in 46 days. Trucking was held back by a dearth of decent roadways until the Great Depression: President Franklin Delano Roosevelt responded to the economic crisis with work-relief programs, the largest of which was road building. The modern age of trucking arrived in 1956, courtesy of President Dwight Eisenhower's Federal Aid Highway Act, the result of which was a nation criss-crossed with superhighways. The entire nation was thrown open to commerce on 18 wheels, and the trucking industry soon became a powerful economic force in its own right: By 1996 it employed 9.5 million people and generated more than $360 billion in annual gross revenue.

Ninety-four percent of today's truckers are men; average age, about 40. An increase in female drivers has been limited largely because long stretches on the road render child care arrangements nearly impossible; many of the new women truckers are empty nesters who join their husbands to drive as a team. But this is no carefree road trip to retirement. From the day you obtain your commercial driver's license, you will remain in constant contact with the authorities. Dave Sweetman carries a three-ring binder filled with an array of permits and fuel-tax forms. Gas tax reciprocity varies from state to state; if you cross a state without buying fuel, you must still pay tax on the fuel you used to cross the state. Get caught overweight, overheight, overwidth, or with the wrong light out and you'll find yourself fined and grounded. Every trucker is required by the federal government to log his activity in fifteen minute increments; computerization, satellite tracking and in-cab monitoring (right down to engine revolutions) is spreading, and while many truckers welcome the simplification, nearly all of them bristle at the idea of some far-off spy in a cubicle tracking every gear they grind.

Today's trucks are wired. In addition to his steering wheel, Dave Sweetman overlooks an array of 19 knobs and 25 gauges. He can summon up screen after screen of performance data. As we course over the ruts and grooves, the easy lurch of the road reaches the seat through the air-ride shocks, and I am reminded of a trucker in Alaska who once told me his cluster of computerized doodads gave him good information, "but 90 percent of it you feel in your ass."

Speaking of which, trucking is not good for your hemorrhoids. Or your back. Or your knees. Or your anatomy in general. If your back doesn't go out after years of jostling by the road, it'll go one day when you're busting your hump to unload 80 pallets of meat before someone poaches your next load, or you'll do your knee jumping off a flatbed, or dropping from the cab. The endless miles set up a craving for coffee and nicotine, and the fats and carbohydrates waiting at every diner set your heart and arteries on twin trajectories eventually intersecting at a stroke.

So much for the body. What about the soul? Truckers will tell you trucking is frequently twinned with loneliness, that if you've got trouble at home, the road gives you time and space to turn it over and over, roll it like a worry wheel, and sometimes you run it down, get it corralled, but more often than not it just wears a deeper groove. Loneliness and distance create their own little market for companionship. At the Nevada line, a warm-voiced woman offers a brief, polite invite over CB channel 19: free hot coffee and free hot showers, available at a place just off the road; additional services, available for a fee. Many trucks sport decals in the image of a reptile stamped with a red circle-and-slash, meaning the driver is not interested in the services of freelance hookers truckers call "lot lizards."

I switch trucks, riding out of Iowa and into Nebraska with Bandit and his wife, Lady Frog. They're pulling two backhoes on a flatbed. Bandit has been assigned to handle public relations for Share America on CB Channel 19, the traditional trucker's virtual hangout. Some good ol' boy calls in, apparently unimpressed: "That convoy stuff, that's a crock a shit." Bandit keys up the mic. "Well I'm sorry you feel that way, sir," he says, his voice like a wood rasp drawn through steel wool. "We're just trying to improve the image of trucking and encourage everyone to make that little extra effort to make our highways and byways safe — if that ain't for you, well, have a safe trip, driver. This is the Bandit, and we're outta sight."

Bandit lights a cigarette. "I smoke too much." He's small but stocky. Ex-military. Loaded with turquoise jewelry. He does smoke too much. His laugh sounds like melted cheese. But he maintains that measured military bearing, a stance that suggests sudden moves are ill-advised. I'm perched in the bunk, and he looks at me in the mirror. "You want something to drink? The fridge is right there. Please — you are at home. Anything." This is a new Freightliner Century. Capacious. You can stand up in the sleeper and still not reach the skylight. The refrigerator is studded with novelty magnets: a Snoopy, a pineapple, a banana, a watermelon, strawberries, grapes, one in the shape of a tooth, several shaped like states. A countertop holds an array of scented candles — one placed atop a doily — a stock of vitamins, and a flowered box of

Scotties tissues. A tapestry of a semi superimposed on the American flag hangs over the bunk, which is loaded with embroidered pillows and stuffed animals. The Trucker's Prayer is clipped to Bandit's sun visor. A solid crucifix is centered over the windshield. This is not a truck. This is a home, a business, a shrine.

I ride with as many truckers as I can: Jim, originally from Frog Jump, Tennessee, who bounced my kidneys across Nevada in a Wal-Mart truck filled with giant orange jack o' lantern leaf bags. He has a part-time gig as an Otis impersonator for *Mayberry R.F.D.* conventions. Lee, 67, running freight with his wife of 46 years, listening to 2500 watts of Pink Floyd and Ravel, stopping at schools to give truck-safety seminars. George, his gorgeous canary-yellow Freightliner Classic grossing 80,000 pounds, loaded with Hidden Valley dressing and Armor All. He loves the road, but misses his two babies and wife back in New Jersey; and, with another baby on the way, he thinks he'll trade the Classic in for a wrecker so he can work close to home. George is training a rookie, Marques, and as we roll under the sun in Wyoming, he tells Marques it takes twice the woman to be a truck driver's wife than it takes a man to be a trucker. The Connecticut Yankee, an ex-policeman loaded with cardboard. He used to drive local, in Long Island. Hated the bumper-to-bumper madness. He waves at the big western sky. "This is like vacation every day." He blames trucking's image troubles on "Billy Big Rigger; the guy who trashes around the truckstop playing video games for two hours, then hammers down the highway trying to make up for lost time." And then there was Thurley, the woman who trucked me in a smaller rig across a numbing stretch of Nebraska. Thurley simply bustles with goodness. "Look at that, look at that!" she kept saying, pointing at yet another wearying flat-line vista. "Praise the Lord. Thank you Jesus." She thanked the Lord every quarter mile. Look, I wanted to say, this really isn't His best work. But that's my problem, not hers.

On the convoy's last night together, we gather in a casino parking lot just inside the Nevada state line. It's a jolly little carnival. Joey Holiday, a singer who does a truckstop tour and bills himself as "The Nation's #1 Trucker Entertainer," unfolds his tiny portable stage, and sings, "She ain't just a truck, Lord, she's my best friend." In between songs he emcees a coin toss to raise money for a child's wheelchair. Above us, the casino marquee — an exploding neon rainbow — grows brighter as the night grows darker. Jim comes out in his Otis clothes, does a ten-minute improv around the fact that he's been driving for two days with a splinter in his butt. The truckers eat it up, guffawing and shaking their heads. I recall these faces a few weeks later when I come across a *Salon* piece in which the writer takes a sarcastic jab at "— those American Trucking Association propaganda films they used to show to high school civics classes. 'Did you know that the clothes in your closet and the food on your table were delivered by truck? That's right. Think about that the next time you see a trucker — and give him a friendly wave!'"

The ATA is hardly impartial, and the road has its share of dangerous, unfriendly truckers. While industry representatives are quick to point out that the number of deadly accidents per mile are down (and have been decreasing steadily since 1980), there are still enough large trucks (4,871 in 1997) involved in fatal crashes to keep groups like Citizens for Reliable and Safe Highways (CRASH) actively lobbying for further restrictions. But: Did you know that the clothes in your closet and the food on your table were delivered by truck? The *Without Trucks, America Stops* slogan is unsophisticated, but we're all complicit in that premise, every single shopping one of us. It is simply not feasible to run train tracks to every grocery store and Wal-Mart in America. Air drops are imprecise and messy, and canals are out of the question. Dave and Bandit and Thurley are on the road to feed our collective habit. We voted them there with our wants and charge cards. Little wonder, then, that they are troubled by our casting them as the heavies.

Tomorrow I will roll into Reno with Dave Sweetman, and his odometer will kick over 2000 miles on the nose, just like he said, and we'll all gather up at the Knights of the Road Truckerfest before embarking on an air horn-blasting parade through downtown Reno. But tonight we're all just hanging out in a parking lot, happy to be truckers.

And 100 yards to the north, out on I-80, the economy rolls on. ◀

▶ Rolling Thunder

In 1988, a small group of Vietnam veterans rode their motorcycles through Washington D.C. to protest the U.S. government's abandonment of prisoners of war and soldiers missing in action. Since then, the protest — known as Rolling Thunder, in reference to the sound of the bikes and the massive bombing campaign carried out during the Vietnam War — has grown to include over 270,000 participants.

Midnight at the The Wall. We enter on an incline, descend past the first thin sliver of names, then edge silently downward to the darkened vertex, the incline running deeper and the sliver widening until the names stretch beyond the reach of a tall man. A smattering of candles flutter along the footpath and set the polished Bangalore marble to gleaming like sheets of black ice. But if you lean in close and turn your head, as if listening for the names, you'll see the candlelight caught in a film of fingerprints. The satin marble face — cool and smooth as lacquer — invites touch. Few people are drawn to the Wall without being drawn to touch it, and the prints are trace elements of this instinctive ritual.

But then your fingertips come to rest on a sandpapery row of etched letters. The letters form a name. You think of the mother then, cradling the baby, speaking that name. Then you conjure a young man's face to match. The image is necessarily incomplete, necessarily ghostly. And then you find yourself wondering what you might have been doing that day in '59, or '68, or '75 when — still young — he fell. The power of the Wall is in those names — a silent roll call grit-blasted into the stone to remind us that we are not honoring an abstraction, we are honoring 58,214 comrades; each with a life, each with a death. Each with a name.

But there are names missing. And so early the next morning, after four hours of sleep, here I am on the tail of an 85th Anniversary Edition Harley-Davidson driven by a sharpshooting ex-Marine everyone calls Murdoch, wind slapping at my ears, rolling up Interstate 66 toward Washington D.C. The sun is risen and the land is green, but it's early, and the cold air stiffens my knuckles. A staggered double line of dancing headlights trails us in the mirror. And running right behind them, looming like the mother ship, is a big black Class 8 Volvo semi tractor. Most of the guys in this motorcade had a hand in building that Volvo as part of UAW Local 2069, and they've brought it with them to help honor the names you don't see on The Wall, the prisoners-of-war and missing-in-action soldiers who never came home.

By 7:45 a.m. we pull into a 58-acre parking lot outside the Pentagon. There are already several thousand bikes in line. It'll be a noisy day. Then I think of the names on the wall, and the names not on the wall, and I think, well, it *oughta* be noisy.

The bikes — Harleys, mostly — roll in for hours, in fits and starts at first, but then in a steady, rumbling stream. By 11 a.m., the overpass leading to the parking lot is swarmed with spectators; like a gaggle of flightless birds, they perch chock-a-block on the railing, flock the sidewalks, and spill down the grassy slope overlooking the swelling sea of cycles below. The bikes are packed cheek-by-jowl, clicking and cooling, canted on their kickstands in ranks roughly ten abreast. Riders milling around on foot lend the scene a sort of constant motion. They check out each other's bikes, snap pictures, reunite with friends. There are a lot of bare arms, a lot of tattoos. A group of eight riders who look like a bad stretch of highway are holding hands and leading each other in prayer. Artie Miller, Rolling Thunder's founder, stands alone in the center of a clear spot, surrounded by lights, cameras and satellite gear, all rigged up in a C-SPAN headset, answering questions none of us can hear. It's overcast now, but warmer. The bikes keep coming.

At high noon a cluster of red, white and blue balloons rises into the air and the parking lot begins to rumble. Beneath me, the seat shudders as Murdoch fires up the Harley. One row over, a long, tall biker with skin to match his leathers pogos up and down on the kick starter of his chopper, a rough hunk of work that looks more like a plumbing project than a motorcycle. He runs out of breath and a buddy strides over to help him. The buddy is heavier, and when he brings his full weight down on the kick bar, the bike backfires, then chugs to life. For a while, while we wait to get moving, the exhaust becomes a little overpowering, but everyone is too keyed up to care.

When we finally swing out toward Arlington Memorial Bridge, and I catch my first glimpse of the spectators, I feel a thrill. And when Murdoch snaps off a salute to a solitary middle-aged Ranger standing at ramrod attention, the thrill turns to tightness in my throat. I get that feeling all along the route.

We swing right at the Lincoln Memorial, rumble up Independence Avenue, hang a left around the Capitol and cruise the home stretch down Constitution Avenue. I remember the trip in glimpses: The family, curbside, holding a homemade sign: *Where is Private Jack Smith?* Clenched fists, raised alongside peace signs. Murdoch exchanging "Hooah!s" with grinning Marines. Kids with flags. A man in fatigues, with a quiet face, just watching. Murdoch rapping the engine, and the echoes splattering back from the government buildings. The smell of overheating engines, hot clutches.

And then it's over. National Park Service police on horses direct us onto the grass of the Mall. Murdoch and I leave the bike, double back and catch a ride on the back of the Volvo. Then we end up sitting in the grass beneath a tree. I remark on the irony of so many Vietnam vets being here, on the very ground where their actions were so vehemently opposed. The protested have become the protesters. He agrees, but points out that many of the original protesters show up to support Rolling Thunder. "They realize the soldiers did what they were told," he says. "They were called, and they went."

In this age of declining postmodern irony, it is fashionable to dismiss such loyalty as gullible foolishness or blind jingoism. But to do so is to deny a cold truth: Vietnam may have been a mistake, but the loyalty of the troops misused there still underpins our very existence. The time will come when it is required again, and if you have grown used to freedom, you better pray someone is still willing to risk theirs for yours. Like it or not, deny it or dismiss it, eventually you need someone willing to do a little dirty work in defense of the ivory tower and the well-groomed suburb. Murdoch and I talk a long time, then walk to The Wall. The bikes are still rolling across the Memorial Bridge.

On Monday, a few of us returned to The Wall for a memorial service. The speakers on the dais were joined by an empty chair draped with a pair of fatigues, a helmet, and a set of boots. It was a reverent coda to the previous day's thunderous remembrance.

When I got back home, I tried to describe the thunder of 270,000 motorcycles, the passion in the peace signs and fists and salutes, and the desolate power of the names, and the empty boots. Mostly people were polite, but their eyes took on that wary glaze we reserve for street preachers and proselytizing relatives, and I had just the faintest taste of what it must have been to return from the jungle in '68 and search for a sympathetic ear.

When you face The Wall at midnight, the Washington monument is all lit up at your back, standing clean as a butcher's bone and solid as a compass pointing the way to Glory. It is a monument to look up to, a monument to remind you of all this country ever hoped to be. The Wall, on the other hand, is cut darkly into the earth. To see The Wall, you have to hunker down and peer into the marble until you find your own face looking out, strung with names. ◄

► A Pilgrim's Progress

I've used up every trick that I had hidden up my sleeve
Think it's time I reconcile with what I had to leave
— Marty Stuart, "Redemption"

The president of the Country Music Foundation — currently serving his third term — is gigging at a casino in Reno. He is following an elephant act. Wayne Newton — in all his black-rinse, bankrupt glory — is working the other end of the hall.

The president in question — Marty Stuart — has become country music's greatest curator. Beginning when he was still a teenager on the bluegrass circuit, Stuart bought one country music-related object per week, from old records to old guitars. Eventually, by his own admission, "it just got out of control." Today, he owns an entire warehouse of country memorabilia, from Hank Williams' hat to Jimmie Rodgers' lantern. But recently, he has become concerned with his own legacy — with the *art* of his craft. He has been seeking, as he says, "a deeper place." Still, he betrays no compunction for performing in the wake of elephants. "I kinda like what Keith Richards says," chuckles Stuart. "He says art is short for Arthur." He continues. "Mom and Pop, or that dude that's worked hard all week, he really don't give a shit about my art collection, or my knowledge of Bill Monroe's first band. He don't care about Charlie Poole. In truth, they are there to be entertained, and we've got to remember: That's the gig."

Stuart is using this nine-day casino stand to work out the particulars of a new set incorporating material from his latest release, a concept album entitled *The Pilgrim*. *The Pilgrim* is one part musical, one part parable, one part tribute, and one part shot at re-demption. Once a precocious disciple of country's hillbilly progeni-tors (he joined Lester Flatt's band at the age of 13 over a quarter century ago, playing rhythm guitar and mandolin), and its iconic outlaws (with stints as Johnny Cash's guitarist and son-in-law), Stuart eventually hit the big time with a solo career in which his musicianship was frequently obscured by couture and coiffure.

At the peak of his fame, Marty Stuart was a rockin' little rooster, prone to conch belts and butt wiggle — an embroideried, hot-pickin' cool-breeze, blowing into town with a Saturday night band to tear things up and move on. Lots of flash and grin, doin' a little thing they called the hillbilly rock. Lester's little boy wonder done gone Nashvegas.

It worked, in a party-hearty sort of way. Still, when you've paid your dues pickin' "Don't Get Above Your Raisin'" for the man who wrote it, but paid for your bus by singing "Touch me, turn me on, and burn me down," you know that somewhere out there ahead of you is a crossroads: One path leads to statesmanlike viability; the other, to geriatric parody.

The Pilgrim grew out of two events: the death of Bill Monroe, and a good book. Stuart was recording at Sun Studios when he got the call about Bill Monroe. He went walking in the back streets of Memphis, and came back with a verse in his head:

> *I am a lonesome pilgrim, far from home*
> *What a journey I have known*
> *I might be tired and weary, but I am strong*
> *Pilgrims walk, but not alone*

He wrote two more verses, played it once for the band, then recorded it in a single take. "For a year and a half, it was the only song I had to show for this project," says Stuart. In the interim, he found himself participating in a series of memorial services: Monroe, Grandpa Jones, Roy Huskey, Jr. Time was passing in the form of friends.

He also read Nicholas Dawidoff's *In The Country of Country*. "That book had as much to do with kickin' this album off in my head as the death of Mr. Monroe," says Stuart. "When you opened it up, there was a map of the United States. And all the towns highlighted were like spiritual touchstones. Tupelo; Meridian; Bakersfield; Rosine, Kentucky; Turkey, Texas. And I noticed I wasn't included in that book, nor should I have been. But it gave me something to strive for. I wanted to go back and dig through all the vines, the myths, the fables, the experiences, everything I had packed on my back for the past 25 years. I wanted to cut through every bit of that and find a place where I could hear the pure holy tones, and hear those ancient voices from that other world. And they're still there. You just gotta go get 'em."

The album is called to order by a train whistle, followed by the sounds of a fidgeting orchestra, tuning while the house lights dim. Then a shimmering glissando spills from the string section, cascading like a clutch of pearls down a spiral staircase, converging with a steam-train snare and the Doppler moan of a steel guitar, the whole works sweeping into a chonkety-chonk rhythm that's all centerline and telephone poles, off to track the troubled path of a pilgrim.

Loosely structured around the true story of a man from Stuart's hometown who killed himself in front of his wife over her infidelity, the album's structure (woven with prelude and reprise, split by a 31-second intermission in the form of the Clinch Mountain Boys' "Cluck Old Hen") draws heavily on Stuart's recent involvement in writing for the stage and screen (Stuart just completed work on a musical by Los Angeles playwright Mary Willard, and wrote and performed the score for the upcoming Billy Bob Thornton film, *Daddy and Them*).

"It really was kind of the training wheels for this album," says Stuart. "Instead of goin' for that mentality of a Tin Pan Nashville song, to where you try in two minutes and thirty seconds to cram every nook and cranny with a hook, I think it taught me just to relax and tell the story, let it flow."

Stuart also cites Roger Miller's *Big River*, the 1985 Tony Award–winning musical based on Mark Twain's *Huck Finn*, as an early seed of inspiration. "I remember when Roger took me upstairs at his house in New Mexico and showed me his briefcase full of manuscripts," says Stuart. "He truly was proud of that work — and I remember thinking, 'Maybe someday I can do a project that has that sort of ambition'." He also did some of the writing in his warehouse, surrounded by the Nudie suits and boots of those who walked before him.

Stuart's story features a range of characters, including the jilted husband, a hobo, a waitress and an omniscient hipster crow. The Pilgrim himself is the unwitting "other man," and the album tracks his attempts to flee the tragedy he set in motion. The story is told by many voices, including Ralph Stanley, Emmylou Harris, and George Jones; thanks in part to the structure of the work, each artist's contribution comes off less as a guest shot than the natural occupation of a role. When Ralph Stanley sings about "a tormented man" his withered voice and ambling banjo foreshadow both the tragedy and the journey. When Johnny Cash appears near the end of the album to deliver an apparitional recitation of Alfred Lord Tennyson's "Sir Galahad," it is as if the grand quatrains are scudding across a lowering Welsh sky.

As a singer, Stuart has always relied more on phrasing and attitude than melodics, and although several cuts on *The Pilgrim* are straightforward hillbilly rockers *a la* 1991's *Tempted*, he allows a song such as "Hobo's Prayer" to unfold with unforced ease, giving story precedence over strut. "The Observations of a Crow" is a laid-back piece of easy humor. And the title song, reappearing in three "acts" over the course of the record, is larger than life — at once glorious and humble, filled with lonesome, touched by gospel, and presented — thanks to the frisson of a splash cymbal here and there — with unabashed theatrics.

And then there are the instruments. Uncle Josh Graves leads out "The Greatest Love of All Time" with a pinging dobro run. Gary Hogue's steel guitar suffuses "Reasons" with an anguish that resurrects the instrument from its relegated status as token Music Row garnish and puts a perfectly straight face on the edgy resignation of the line, "It was the perfect excuse to buy bullets." Conversely, on "Goin' Nowhere Fast," Hogue lets the steel skip along beneath the driving drums and big guitars, beep-beeping like a little red Nash delighted to be part of the convoy.

Throughout the album runs Stuart's 1933 Lloyd Loar Gibson F–5 mandolin. Writers often describe the sound of a mandolin as "chiming," but in Stuart's hands, the instrument is most effective providing more contemplative accents — to wit, the delicate avian flutters on "The Pilgrim," and "The Greatest Love of All Time." "For me, the mandolin has been a magic wand," says Stuart. "I can do 'Burn Me Down,' and then pick up a mandolin and sing 'Dark as a Dungeon,' and my credibility to myself comes back instantly."

Marty Stuart got the pickin' bug while growing up in the Deep South town of Philadelphia, Mississippi. "Daddy really liked stringband music, and the first record I ever got, when I was five, was Flatt & Scruggs." Shortly thereafter, the Flatt & Scruggs television show debuted. "It brought those songs to life in a new way. And for me and Daddy, that was our quality time. We'd sit and watch country music together."

But there was a subplot. "This was when all the civil rights business was goin' down," he says. "Racial relations were horrible. The entire mood 'round our town was chaos. And the whole nation was breathin' down our neck. Daddy took me and my sister down, we parked his truck, and Jennifer and me stood on the hood of the truck as Martin Luther King marched his Freedom March through town. This whole town was crazy. And in the middle of all that darkness, to sit down at the end of the week and have Flatt & Scruggs come on and pick some tunes for you, it was like the cloud lifted. There was a ray of light that came in with them. They were like your favorite country cousins."

The final track on the new album, "Mr. John Henry, Steel Driving Man," is a two-minute instrumental by Marty and Earl Scruggs. "I had no plan for that to be on the record," says Stuart, "but it took me full circle, to when I was a kid standin' in front of that television set. And it brought it back, in my opinion, to a point of pure art, pure enjoyment, pure fun, pure credibility. One microphone, sittin' knee to knee, just goin' for it. And it goes back to points in my life — whether I was going through a divorce, or gettin' my sanity back, or just road-fried, or whatever the situation, happy times or bad times — a trip to Earl's house, and a good pickin' over at Scruggs', you just come out feelin' different. It's like goin' to church or something."

Stuart's first real musical instruction came from a teenager named Carl Jackson. "He was a child prodigy," says Stuart. "He played on the Grand Ole Opry with a group called Jim & Jesse & the Virginia Boys. When Carl would come back from Nashville to work on his schoolwork, he and his Dad would come down to my hometown and play. And I heard about Carl Jackson, so I went and met him, and his Dad — this was when I was 11 — and his Dad recognized the fire in my eyes, and bein' that he'd already raised one musical kid, he kinda took me under his wing and helped me, showed me my first little bits on the mandolin, taught me a couple of fiddle tunes and stuff. He got me started." At home, Stuart tutored himself with an adjustable-speed phonograph. "I'd take records and slow'em down, so I could get the licks, then speed it up and play along."

At 12, Stuart met Bill Monroe, who handed him a pick and challenged him to go learn how to use it. A year later, the boy waylaid Lester Flatt backstage and asked for a job. He got it, and his education began in earnest. "Out there on the circuit, I just basically had access to anybody's playin' that I liked. They were usually the kind of guys that I could go up to. Vassar Clements, for instance: 'Vassar, I love the way you play this, how do you do this?' And country music musicians are really friendly that way for the most part; they'll sit down and work it out with you."

Even as a child, Stuart claims he never had any doubts about his career choice. In pictures from the era, he is a half-pint in a suit coat and a straw cowboy hat ("No matter what I did, I came out lookin' like Eddie Munster," he jokes), stepping right up front for his solos, respectful of his elders, but hardly deferential.

The first time he played the Opry, he fell asleep as Lester drove him to town. "Lester thought I'd be uptight and nervous," says Stuart, "but I never have been. It was totally what I prepared myself for. It was what I wanted to do; I knew who I was with, and I knew the importance of the gig. About two weeks in, on the way home from doing a Martha White radio show one day, I was thinkin', 'Hey man, you're doin' pretty good,' and the next thing I heard in my head was, 'Now see if you can keep the gig!'" He laughs. He kept the gig and got others, including work for Clements and Doc Watson.

So how did he wind up doing pay-per-views with Travis Tritt? "When I was starvin', and nobody paid any attention to anything I was doin', back in the late 80s, I was cuttin' country songs, rockabilly songs — and actually, I was at a point, I was tryin' to find myself, too. I was out exploring musically. And the thing that hit for me was a song called 'Hillbilly Rock.' That was a conjured-up piece of business, and it was fun, and it was enjoyable, and it took off. And so I tried to keep up with it and help promote it. But it got to a point where I was goin', 'It's not ringin' as true as it once did to me.' I don't think I was guilty of anything, other than tryin' to keep up with what I had created. I think what I was more guilty of than anything is not walkin' away from that particular thing six months earlier. But I don't really apologize for it. It served me well, and I think it rings true for what it was."

"You've got to remember, too, from the standpoint of a hardcore purist point of view, that Lester's band, we were looked upon as commercial whizzes, say, compared to Ralph Stanley, who was a more pure mountain tone, or Doc Watson, or the old-time, hardline folkies. They looked at us as like a commercial Opry band, instead of the pure thing that I look back upon it as sometimes. In bluegrass and old-time music and folk music, there's always been that dividing line, what Dylan put up with at Newport.

"To this day, you go back to the world of bluegrass, you'll probably find those that despise Alison Krauss, and think she's totally commercial, and prefer a more old-time sound, but then again she's brought a lot of people to the format. And I'm sure Steve Earle singing bluegrass infuriates a lot of old bluegrass hardliners, but once again, it brings a whole lot of light to Del McCoury, and vice versa."

As president of the CMF, Stuart has frequently and publicly chided country music for abandoning its ancestry, and he remains critical of country music's commercial state — with one confounding qualification: "I'm guilty of helpin' it get there," he confesses. "But there comes a time when you just have to walk away from any gimmicks — in my case, bein' a rhinestone cowboy. No matter what kind of ass-whippin' I'm about to get out there commercially.

"I tried to keep it happy and light for years. That's the way I was consulted and advised and researched to do it. But the thing I miss about country music is the stories. The first country music hit was 'The Prisoner's Song,' and before that that I loved Pop

Stoneman's 'Sinking of the Titanic,' recorded in the '20s. Folk and country singers used to be correspondents. Woody Guthrie, when he'd sing to us about Grand Coulee Dam, sing those folk songs, 'Deportee,' those kinds of things — he was a correspondent. George Jones was a great correspondent of broken hearts; Johnny Cash, Merle Haggard, they all were great reporters, and somewhere along the line, the demographics changed, and it just got to be about sellin' ice cream cones on a radio station.

"But if you really get out and walk the sidewalks and the country roads of this world, you find out that the same problems still exist out there and there's a lot of tragedy, and everybody's told not to talk about it anymore. It's OK to make movies about it, but don't sing songs about it. Well, that's a buncha shit.

"This *Pilgrim* thing, for the most part, there's so much truth in the darkness and the tragedy of it, and I find that when I stand flat-footed and sing "Reasons" with an honest heart onstage, people understand it."

And what about the songs that paid for the bus? "I think there comes a point for certain kinds of songs when you outgrow'em, and you just have to say, 'Man, you were my friend, but I don't expect you to do that for me anymore — you shouldn't expect me to do that for *you* anymore!" He laughs. "Still, Mick Jagger probably hates to sing 'Satisfaction,' but when I go see the Stones, I'd be disappointed if I didn't hear it. Johnny Cash told me once, 'I had no idea "A Boy Named Sue" was gonna do what it did — when you cut a song, you better be ready to sing it for the rest of your life'."

"It's a total playground to me out here," Stuart summarizes, surveying the seemingly contradictory landscape of country music he roams from one day to the next. "Last week me and Uncle Josh Graves and Earl Scruggs did a recording, I sang a spiritual at the funeral of the father of one of the Fairfield Four — he was an old Chess artist and I was the only white boy in that place —

and Saturday night I played at a Reno hotel where I had an elephant act as an opener and Wayne Newton on the other end of the hall. It's like one of the most crazy adventures I could ask for."

Perhaps you've read those *Sports Illustrated* profiles, detailing an athlete's rise, fall and recovery, the ones that end with the jock out of rehab, back on the field and in the hands of Jesus, the ones that conclude on the upbeat, setting you up nicely for the announcement on "SportsCenter" a week later that the subject was arrested after blowing out his knee wrestling a transvestite hooker for a bag of crack behind a dumpster. We have learned to mistrust neatly-wrapped tales of epiphany and redemption, and should.

There is redemption in *The Pilgrim*; it is a solid, uplifting work of informed intent. But the Arty Marty is not prepared to disband the Marty Party. The rhinestone cowboy is right there in the wings, as much a part of the irreconcilable contradictions as the mandolin and the elephants. Marty Stuart isn't renouncing anything — and you get the feeling he knows this. He won't be pulling a Cat Stevens any time soon. The clothes are still by Manuel. The hair is still a salt-and-pepper brushfire. He's never completely out of earshot of the carnival barker, and he doesn't mind. He hears the voices muttering about squandered talent, the critics who suggest he has preserved more of country's heritage with his warehouse than with his music. But *The Pilgrim* sounds as if the journey has been more keenly observed than the tight pants might suggest. And when he comes in off the playground, grabs his mandolin, and knocks on Earl Scruggs' door, Earl lets him right on in there. ◄

▶ Farther Along: A Eulogy for Grandpa Jones

Roughly 30 years ago, before the methodologies of holistic health care and the vagaries of corporate cost-cutting convened a dialectic that produced today's burgeoning home health care industry, my mother — then a young nurse in a small rural hospital — was recruited by the county to be on night call for a dying 92-year-old woman whose family had promised to keep her out of the nursing home. The house was remotely located, and the woman's son, Henry, usually called after dark, so rather than send Mother alone, we'd pack our family of five into the Rambler, and Dad would pilot us through the swamps and backcountry to where the small wooden house sat hunched in the trees at the end of a short dirt drive. I was very young — not yet four — but I remember wolfish dogs looming through the moonlight, some tethered to brush-bound Packards, others circling the Rambler, stopping to strain at the windows.

Usually we waited with Dad in the car — uneasily, I remember — but at least once I followed Mom inside. I remember shadows, more dogs, a cousin in the corner, a dissembled engine on the kitchen table. I remember Henry ushering us in, solicitous and polite, but always with a bit of the mad scientist's assistant about him. The nursing arrangement ended in late summer, Henry's mother died shortly thereafter, and I don't recall ever seeing Henry again. For three decades the dogs and trees and old cars distilled themselves into a handful of images — a moon-soaked hillbilly gothic.

I walked up that driveway again last month, this time in full volunteer firefighter's gear. The day before, Henry, in his 80s now, had called some neighbors, said he was having trouble with his

furnace. Later, someone saw smoke, and called the fire department. When they arrived, and fought their way inside, they found
Henry on the floor. It looked like he might have gone back in to
unchain one of his gang of dogs. Whatever the case, he lay dead,
two dogs draped over his body as if to shield him from the flames.
I was gone the day of the fire, but when it re-ignited the next day,
I was part of the small crew that returned.

Oftentimes the only way to completely extinguish an exten-
sive fire is to pull the structure apart, and so after we chopped and
sprayed and sweated most of the morning, a backhoe was called
in. Slowly and implacably the articulated steel arm drew and quar-
tered the house, and as each scoop swung past, we soaked it down.

In dying, the old house gave up a lot of history. Beneath the
shabby, weatherbeaten exterior, patched and teetering with trash,
were signs of a grander time: a hand-turned pilaster, the rem-
nants of a parlor. Deeper still, the original body of the house was a
bulwark of hand-squared and fitted logs. And tumbling from scoop
after scoop of sodden ashes, signs of something even more surprising: the skeleton of a banjo, the pleated bellows of an accordion,
the shell of a mandolin, bits of a Victrola. And records. Stacks of
them, thick and vintage, some melted, some expanded and separated into layers, others apparently pristine. I knew Henry had
been a mechanic, knew he had mowed cemeteries, but I had never
heard anything about the music.

"Oh yeah," said one of the firemen, "he gave lessons in the old
days." Later that week someone stopped in the implement store
where my brother works and allowed as how Henry could "play
anything with strings." I looked up Henry's closest surviving relative. He told me Henry's heros were Mac and Bob, the two blind
singers who were a mainstay on WLS through 1950, and whose
"When the Roses Bloom Again," was a hit in 1926. He also favored
the work of Lulu Belle & Scotty, the husband-and-wife team on
the WLS *National Barn Dance* from 1934 to 1958. A local man

who still picks bluegrass and country gospel for church groups and nursing home residents told me how Henry taught him licks as a child: "He'd give you fundamentals, get that metronome going. He had a down-to-earth style."

Right before we rolled the hose up and headed home that afternoon, a Grandpa Jones album tumbled out atop a pile of ash and old bedsprings. Louis "Grandpa" Jones died three days later.

In 1929, at the age of 16, Louis Marshall Jones billed himself as "The Young Singer of Old Songs." Talk about hip — 60 years prior to alternative country, Jones was already doing the retro thing. At the age of 22, his co-host on a morning radio show accused him of being slow and grouchy; of acting like a grandpa. The name stuck, and with the addition of high-topped boots, fake mustache, wire-rimmed spectacles and bright suspenders, so did the schtick.

Singing and frailing on his banjo, Jones worked the radio show circuit, formed a gospel quartet with Merle Travis in the '40s, and made his first appearance on the Grand Ole Opry in 1946. He had a handful of hits, and was inducted into the Country Music Hall of Fame in 1978. Most of my generation came to know him through "Hee Haw," of course, and he remained with the show until its end in 1992.

While most performers cling to their youth, Grandpa eased into old age like he'd been waiting for it all his life. He gave his last performance at the Opry in January of 1998; he died February 19th at age 84. When I heard, I thought of that album on the ash pile, and those banjo skeletons. It struck me as coincidence more than karma, but it did set me to thinking about these two lives lived over the same eight decades: Grandpa carving out a career that sustained him but didn't consume him, Henry living his idiosyncratic loner's life, refusing the company of anyone but his dogs, the indignity of his position outshone by the dignity of his choice.

Beyond the "Hee Haw" clowning, beyond the reclusive old man with his dogs and beached Packards, were two men who found joy in the same pure sounds, whose fingers could coax living history from the strings. For a few days, I despaired over Henry's lost recordings and instruments. But the more I pondered it, the more I found a kind of holiness in the idea of all that music just rising into the air, leaving nothing to be picked over by mortals. If I despair anything, I despair that for 30 years, I lived within a short Rambler ride of a man who could teach mountain music, but in the end, with the old days eclipsed by noise, had no takers. ◄

▶ The Osmotic Elvis

The first thing I remember about Elvis is that he was dead. The news was postdated, and obtained in oblique fashion, but that, as it turns out, is precisely the point where Elvis and I are concerned. The Elvis I know has almost nothing to do with albums or films and almost everything to do with saturation and assimilation. I never went looking for him, never bought his music, never watched his movies. He filtered down and found me. In all his mutable states — the thin Elvis, the fat Elvis; the Army Elvis, the Vegas Elvis; the hero, the has-been — to many of my generation he is simply the osmotic Elvis.

When I learned Elvis was dead, I didn't get the news from the news. I got it from a television commercial. I was visiting a friend, and as we passed through his living room — two thirteen-year-olds headed out for another game of h-o-r-s-e — an announcer was promoting an Elvis tribute show to be held on a local radio station. An image of a man with a microphone appeared on the screen in silhouette. As the spot concluded, the image faded, and the announcer's voice, tremulous with a touch of reverb, called the name three times: "Elvis? . . . Elvis? . . . Elvis?" I remember I thought the spot overwrought. And I remember we went about our basketball untroubled that the King was dead.

But the osmosis was underway.

In 1991, profoundly recalcitrant country artist Steve Earle recorded the live album *Shut Up and Die Like an Aviator*. Earle was on a grungy downhill slide at the time, the heroin in his veins approaching a lazy terminal velocity. He would shortly be homeless, then incarcerated. He sang like a man forcing up crushed glass. After several encores, the audience whistled for more, but the show was over. As the audio fades, an announcer intones, "Ladies and gentlemen, Steve Earle has left the building." At first listen, I recognized it immediately for what it was: A postmodern invocation drawn on the departed King of Rock 'n' Roll.

Just lately, I've realized something else: I've never heard that quote in its original context. I am familiar with the lexicon, hip to the meaning, but only in a second-hand sense. But that's the thing about the King: You didn't have to be there to "get" Elvis. He gets you.

In June of 1988, Kalamazoo housewife Louise Welling told Pete Cooke of the *Weekly World News* that she saw Elvis in the Burger King. "I'm not an Elvis fan," she said. "I don't have any Elvis records or Elvis books. I'm not into Elvis." But she knew Elvis when she saw him.

I know how she feels. I'm not into Elvis either. Don't have his records, don't have his books. But as the philosophomorical songwriter Mojo Nixon once sang, "Elvis is everywhere." You can't ignore Elvis. He saturates the periphery of our existence. I've never seen the '68 comeback special, but I've seen the commercial for the video, and I've seen the slick magazine ad for the commemorative plate. I know it's hip to respond to the mention of a "velvet Elvis" with an arch grin, but I'm not sure why. When it comes to Elvis, I feel like a man who knows all the punch lines, but never really got the joke.

And therein lies a defining Elvis dilemma: Why does a man who evokes jokiness continue to reign supreme in American cultural lore? If he is such a clown, why is he still King? If a guy like me knows so little about Elvis, why do I have such a *sense* of Elvis?

Elvis died debauched, dissolute, and in a humiliating posture. Where dying is a means to mystique, he died poorly, compared, say, to Marilyn Monroe, perhaps his closest iconic equivalent. Elvis did some decaying long before they put him in his grave, and everyone had a chance to watch. But all the ugly details — the grocery list of drugs, the cheeseburgers, the tumble from the toilet —

did nothing to stop the spread of Elvis. Mythologizing was out-paced only by merchandising. Both continue apace. The King is dead, but the King still sells, and so, long lives the King. It's diffi-cult to focus a search for the source of this perpetuity. There are, as one Web site currently puts it, A Thousand Points of Elvis.

He wasn't the first rock star. Some say that was Bill Haley, and Little Richard would have something to say about *that*. No, rock 'n' roll was ready and waiting for Elvis. He rode it like the ride it was, but it was moving when he got on, and it moved even faster when he got off. Shoot, some say the rock 'n' roll went out of Elvis as far back as '58, the day his hair hit the floor of an Army barbershop. It's an important point: We call Elvis the King of Rock 'n' Roll, but that title alone fails to explain his perennial perva-siveness.

In "The Academic Elvis," Simon Frith says, "his fame was de-pendent on the new mass media of television, Top 40 radio, the teen magazine, the LP. . . ." It is a valid point, but requires expan-sion. I was the firstborn grandchild on both sides of the family. My baby scrapbook bulges with stacks of film and copious notations documenting my precocious aptitudes. My brother followed in two years. His scrapbook is well-stocked but comparatively slim. A second brother arrived three years later. A few pages into the scrap-book, it is as if he stopped developing. The rest of the pages are empty. Today's latter-born celebrities can command media satura-tion Colonel Parker could only dream of, but our interest is di-luted. Elvis was our mass-media firstborn, and we have never kept such a scrapbook since.

But what if you reduce mass media in the equation? Aside from a scratchy 45 of "Heartbreak Hotel," I don't recall hearing Elvis in our house. I suppose I read about him in the paper, but we never had a television, and I know Elvis was dead two years before I had a radio.

Radios were forbidden in our home, but in November of 1979, I discovered one squirreled away in a mysterious slope-roofed closet upstairs in our old farmhouse. I've been able to backtrack the date because when I plugged it in, turned it on, and the tubes warmed, I heard Kermit the Frog, singing his way to #25 on *Kasey Kasem's Top 40* with "Rainbow Connection."

Long before I heard Kermit, back when I was tiny, my brother and I stood in front of my grandma's fireplace, playing what would one day be called "air guitar" while mouthing along to an LP she had put on for the evening. I must have been particularly animated, because my grandma, then in her late 50s, said, "You move like Elvis Presley!"

I didn't even know who Elvis Presley was. And yet, by that time, the moves that had gotten Elvis' pelvis banned in prime time had become *de rigueur* in rock. As limited as my exposure to music and television was, a little drop of Elvis had trickled down and hit me in the hips.

The osmotic Elvis is not always obvious. You see someone owning the stage, shaking his pelvis and whatever else, and you'll be excused for saying, oh, Elvis started all that. You'd be wrong — he didn't start it, he popularized it — but you'd be excused. But then you see a man like Townes Van Zandt, a frail alcoholic ephemera out of Austin, Texas, dead this year at 52, teetering on the edge of a stool, singing the troubled, introspective songs that made him a legend but didn't make him happy, and you hear him tell the story of how it was Elvis on TV with his guitar and Cadillacs and girls that made Townes ask his daddy for his first guitar. Suddenly you think, if Elvis started this man — the utter anti-Elvis — what else did he start?

Before Elvis was everywhere, he was everything. He was whatever you needed him to be. The dangerous erotic rocker, the good and loyal GI, the grandiose balladeer, the film star, the *nouveau riche* hick, the Cadillac philanthropist, the strung-out goofball, the prayerful gospel singer, the bloated postmodern icon. He was a national "local boy does good," he was an archetypical cautionary tale. Here he was in 1956, according to John Shepherd, "eminently successful in flouting the propriety of middle-class sensibilities" with his nationally-televised gyrations. There he was in 1971, sideburned-cheek-by-shadowy-jowl with none other than Richard Nixon, who presented the most famous addict in America with an enameled shield making him an agent of the Bureau of Narcotics and Dangerous Drugs. The irony hits you like an envelope full of pills. The rebel sold out. Officially, symbolically, and to Richard Nixon no less. Little wonder that two weeks after Elvis died, Lester Bangs wrote, "I see him as being more like the Pentagon, a giant armored institution nobody knows anything about except that its power is legendary."

But this bizarre alignment says as much about Elvis' ability to broaden his audience demographic as the artistic range between "Hound Dog" and "Old Shep." How do you like me now, Elvis always seemed to be saying, and what would you like me to be next? He gave us so many ways to remember him, we couldn't forget him. Even if we missed him the first time around.

The future looks good for Elvis. Things will only get better; his image is bound to improve. The whole postage stamp thing was a good omen. It was a highly official way of saying, well, gosh, I think we've made fun of his collars long enough, let's let him slim down and dump the jumpsuit for some vintage lamé.

Applying the Sinatra corollary, we can assume that were Elvis alive today, he would be consigned to embarking on a Mobius strip of farewell/comeback tours, interrupted at regular intervals by celebrity tribute mawkfests. Instead, he's still the sexy shakin' Hillbilly Cat, legal tender backed by the full faith and power of the

United States government. And by God, if there's one thing we love in America, it's eternal youth with a fat wallet.

And then, in the mitigation category, we have become inured to celebrity misbehavior. Elvis and his penchant for panty-clad wrestling girls offended 1950s sensibilities, but the year he died Sid Vicious and the Sex Pistols lurched into America. By October of 1978, Vicious was charged with stabbing his girlfriend to death; four months later, Vicious himself was dead. Shooting one's television suddenly seemed positively quaint.

But one need not pick on punk rockers to define deviancy downward. In the twenty years since Elvis pitched forward to glory, a score of his exploits have been eclipsed by any number of our most favored televangelists. In the end, the fact that Elvis lacked Mick Jagger's metabolism and Keith Richards' liver allowed him to mount a posthumous comeback the Jims — Bakker and Swaggart — can only pray for.

And perhaps the academics — frequently loath, embarrassed, or unable to judge him as an artist — will let down their hair and let Elvis climb up the ivory tower. Some recent readings have been redemptive, and there has been a trend toward analyzing Elvis the Performer rather than Elvis the Myth, Elvis the Meretricious Primitive, Elvis the Snacker.

Strange as it may seem, it may take the demise of Elvis' original legions of fans to pave the path to complete ensconcement. In his own redemptive work, "The Academic Elvis," Simon Frith suggests that "as arguments about performance and identity begin to inform cultural studies, so *perhaps Presley will at last be taken more seriously than his fans* [italics mine]." From this one can infer all that unstinting, uncritical worship made the woolly-heads nervous. I mean, it's not like you've got entire conventions of Beethoven impersonators.

But of course the impersonators won't go away soon, and the sightings won't stop, and some summer, years from now, you'll be stuck in traffic in a strip-mall chunk of town, and the sun will be unforgiving, and right outside your passenger door window will be some guy set up on half a service station parking lot, selling velvet in a frame, and five or six of those beauties will feature the King of Rock 'n' Roll.

Whether the academics decide to elevate him or not, low culture will keep Elvis alive. Everything "Elvis" is a tribute. Even the embarrassments: the tick-tock clocks that dance, the Elvis shampoo. If I am wrong, and *academe* turns on him, all the better. The more vitriolic or condescending the observations, the more they stand tribute to an insatiable need to establish the proper position of the icon, to the power of the icon to evoke.

Do you doubt that Elvis can still evoke? I share my first name with two of the most recognized men in the world: Michael Jackson and Michael Jordan. No one ever makes the association. But if your name is Elvis, you cannot *escape* the association. I have no acquaintances named Elvis, although I can think of a few well-known Elvii: Elvis Grbac, the NFL quarterback; Elvis Costello, the musician; and Elvis Stojko, the champion figure skater. But here's the thing: The first time I heard these names, and the last time I heard them, I thought immediately of Elvis Presley. What other name triggers that instant connection? Adolf, maybe. Jesus, certainly. There was a time, I suppose, when people named their boy Elvis because they liked the name, or they had an uncle Elvis who was dear to the family and got kicked in the head by a mule. But somewhere along the line the boy from Tupelo, Mississippi, stole that name forever, and no one else can ever truly have it for their own. You take that name, you live with a legend.

Make no mistake. The legend lives, but the man is gone. I have it on good authority from Nashville reporter and Graceland–wake attendee Bill Hance that Elvis is indeed dead ("I done seen him"), and posthumous rehab can only do so much. Julie Baumgold drove that point home with just one backhanded line in a gentle, looping dance of an essay written for *Esquire* in 1995. Describing an all-star musical tribute to Elvis, she wrote, "Tributes can be dangerous things, because sometimes all they prove is that it takes forty performers to not quite recall one Elvis."

But then, who needs Elvis back? Elvis was big, but the trickle-down Elvis is culturally colossal. The feeding frenzy took place decades ago, but the postprandial Elvis is very much in demand.

And forever available. ◄

▶ Ramblin' Jack Elliott

To ask Ramblin' Jack Elliott a question is to tug at a snag in a sweater, only to see the yarn unpurl of its own volition, dropping in aimless loops, curling and snaking itself into a variegated fable. Every answer is a folk tale. Conversation is an exercise in free association, switchbacks, good-humored evasion, meanders, and box canyons. Ramblin' Jack Elliott does his talking without aid of a compass.

I have him on the phone. "We're gettin' ready to go to Oregon in the Mercedes," he says. He's at his home in rural California. The Mercedes is a '75. He bought it very used and has had trouble with it. ". . . and I left the window open overnight on my side, because I was bein' the passenger, and I was kind of tired of the rain, and it stopped rainin', and I was enjoyin' the fresh air, while Jan was drivin' us home from our town, and so the sheepskin seat cover got totally soaked. So now I got the electric heater out of my motor home, with an extension cord from the house that runs into one of the back windows on the lee side of the car, it's open about two inches to let the wire come in, and I've got this heater on the floor on an upside down aluminum pot so as to prevent any heat from gettin' in the carpet and settin' fire to the car, and it's aimed up at the seat, from about oh, a foot away from it, from underneath the dashboard on the passenger side, 'cause I couldn't get the damned sheepskin off, it's locked on by the [he adopts a Colonel Klink accent, and begins to yell] Mercedes-Benz head rest, vitch iss heldt in place by two vertical chrome-plated, nine millimeter *shtalks!*"

I haven't asked him a question yet. Already the yarn is coming loose.

Ramblin' Jack Elliott, *Cliffs Notes* version: Bob Dylan is Jack Elliott is Woody Guthrie. "He sounds more like me than I do," goes the Woody Guthrie quote. They busked around the country. When Woody's rambles ended in a decade-long terminal hospital stop, Jack took Woody's walk, talk and music back to the road. Returning to Woody's hospital room one day, Jack met a boy named Bob Dylan bedside. Taught him some things. Soon, Dylan was getting more gigs. Sometimes the marquee read, "Son of Jack Elliott."

Ramblin' Jack Elliott, *Who's Who* version: Jack Kerouac, James Dean, Johnny Cash, Waylon and Willie, Sam Shepard, Jack Nicholson, Rod Stewart, Townes Van Zandt, Kris Kristofferson, Jackson Browne, Greg Brown, Keith Richards, Allen Ginsberg, Ian Tyson, Robert Duvall, Elton John, Paul McCartney, Bruce Springsteen, Doc Watson. All listed as fans or registered acolytes. Mick Jagger left a Ramblin' Jack show in England and bought his first guitar.

But I'm setting him up like a historical figure. He is very much alive. Very much contemporary. Ramblin' Jack Elliott, recent history version: *South Coast,* Grammy, 1995, Best Traditional Folk Album; *Kerouac's Last Dream*, re-issued 1997. And now, *Friends of Mine*, partnering Jack with a telling array: Arlo Guthrie, Peter Rowan, Rosalie Sorrels, Tom Waits, Emmylou Harris, Nanci Griffith, Jerry Jeff Walker, Guy Clark, Bob Weir. On songs written by Joe Ely, Gene Autry, Townes Van Zandt, Jerry Garcia, Merle Travis. And Woody Guthrie and Bob Dylan.

I'm supposed to find out what Jack's got to say about *Friends of Mine*. It's not going to be easy.

Ramblin' Jack Elliott, calling from a hotel in Minneapolis. His voice is tired, all stooped over. He's in the midst of a racking cold. It's late autumn, chill and raining. He wants some fresh air. "But there's this musician-proof window, a suicide-proof window," he grieves. "If you want air you push a button. They charge you for air."

He's in his 60s now. A good age, I suppose, for a folk singer. He's been through the '60s before, hitch-hiking, singing, riding around Woodstock on motorcycles with Bob Dylan and Joan Baez. But tonight he feels old. His hip is acting up. His guitar didn't make the trip. His companion Jan had to stay behind. Tonight he'll play the Cedar Cultural Center.

I mention Peterbilts. He brightens.

Later, he crosses the wooden floor of the Cedar Cultural Center with a slanted amble that bespeaks old injuries, helping himself along with a subtle hike of the elbows. When he stands backstage, it's usually with his hat in hand, his hips hitched, his wiry legs planted in a stance amenable to forking a bronc or straddling the roll of a ship's deck.

At 15, Elliott Charles Adnopoz took the subway out of Brooklyn and joined the rodeo. Tonight, in a ribbed and bibbed shirt, his neck nestled in a bandana you could nap under, he looks every inch the seasoned hand. Young Master Adnopoz is lost to legend. In his place, a troubadour.

The word is too grand, too affected, to suit the man, but the definition is spot-on. From Brooklyn to Britain, from Woody to Waylon, by horse, by ship, by truck, from the '50s to the millennium, he has never stopped covering ground. Singing and moving.

And so now there he is, on the stage of the Cedar Cultural Center, sound-checking a borrowed guitar, playing to the folding chairs on a wet night in the state where Bob Dylan was born.

An assignment landed me on country singer Marty Stuart's tour bus in Petaluma, California, last year. Someone knocked on the door with a note. *Ramblin' Jack is here, wonders if he can come back.* Name meant nothing to me. I got up to leave. "Oh man, no," said Marty Stuart. "You don't know who Ramblin' Jack is? You've *got* to talk to him. He was Woody's cat!"

Ramblin' Jack boarded the bus, hat in hand. "Man, I got something to show you!" said Marty. He disappeared into the back of the bus. In a little bit, he returned with a videotape. An old dub of "The Johnny Cash Show." He popped it in, and there was Ramblin' Jack, twenty-some years younger, different glasses, different hat. Elliott scoffed at the hat, but you could see he was delighted with the footage.

Back when Stuart was playing in Cash's band, Elliott joined them for a brief California tour. In addition to singing and playing, he traded off at the wheel of a Peterbilt with a curly-haired guy he remembers only as Wirehead. They were hauling Cash's sound equipment. "We got on I-5 after our coffee, and I started drivin'. And he says to me as I was goin' through the gears, 'Hey Jack, you ever get one of these long wheel-base trucks off the road?' And I said, 'Why gee, no, I haven't. How come you say that? Are they kind of squirrely?' And he said, 'Just keep it on the road,' and he went in the sleeper."

Marty has to leave for meet-and-greets. He introduces me to Jack first. Talk to this man, he says. For the next two hours, I am educated by way of parable and digression. Kindly and attentively, as though he were the one lucky to be there, Ramblin' Jack Elliott talked of 13-speed split shifts, good horses, the trim of a schooner, and the feel of a stiff guitar pick. He told me about "Muleskinner Blues," and later he joined Marty on stage and sang it. "What key do you do it in?" asked Marty, back on the bus, prior. "A or E, I can't remember," said Jack. "Don't worry, we'll find ya," says Marty.

Then Jack says he called Guy Clark to say hello late last year, and Townes Van Zandt was on the phone. Townes is dead six months now, and at the mention of his name, the talk turns softer. The road manager checks in, asks about Jack sitting in for two songs. "We ain't fer sure of the key yet," says Jack. "Don't worry," says Marty. "You pick one. We'll blunder in behind ya. Always wanted to be in your band."

Anyway, country rocker Marty Stuart and old folkie Ramblin' Jack Elliott: You've heard of the six degrees of Kevin Bacon? With Ramblin' Jack, *two* degrees is *rara avis*.

Back on the phone to California. Still not getting to the point, but having a good time avoiding it. Jack reins in a story, tries to do the proper interview thing.

"Y'wanna talk about guitar chords? Or picks? Tricks? Cases? Airlines?" You see how it goes.

Jan, in the background. Saying something that ends with ". . *new album!*"

"Album!" Jack snickers like a kid hiding from his mother on his night to do dishes.

I take a shot. "Here's the trouble: My editor and your producer will at some point probably expect that we mention the new album, huh?"

"What magazine is this for?"

"*No Depression* magazine."

"Oh, right, *No Depression* magazine . . . that's cute."

I press on, none too eloquently. "Which actually, before I ask you about the album stuff, I think, that magazine is, y'know, it's a young audience, it's kinda alternative country is what it is. How d'you. . ." Jack pulls in without signaling, cuts me off with a whopping *non sequitur*.

"Yeah, I was surprised, because I always got depressed when I was in Seattle, even when I was truckin'. Oh, I like the boats, I love the water up there. I had a wonderful adventure rowin' around in a rubber raft on Lake Union one day, and got picked up by a kid in a lifeboat who was sailing with a homemade sail rig, made out of a transparent piece of visqueen plastic sheet, a two-by-four for a mast, and some clothesline for riggin', and he was steerin' with an oar, he didn't even have a rudder, but it was a real old, tiny little ship's lifeboat off of some ferry boat, and he lived with his parents on some 45-foot yawl that was moored over the yacht anchorage at the opposite side of the bay — the upwind end of this Lake Union, which is full of all kinds of interesting ships. There's a big four-masted lumber schooner that lives there called the *Wawona*, there's the Center for Wooden Boats. . . ."

Which reminds me. All that talk about the stooped-over voice, the colds, the bad hip, I've made him sound old. But when he really gets going, when he's trying to explain to you how that racing schooner he boarded in Guam gathered up the wind and simply *disdained* the water, he drops the cowhand growl and just plain *enthuses*. And when he laughs — usually at a respectful distance following his own observations — it's one of those half-and-half laughs. Half humor, half wonderment at it all. Like, can you *believe* this life?

I'll skip ahead. Tell you that Ramblin' Jack never did get around to commenting on the album. About the time my tape was running out, he announced that *Friends of Mine* producer Roy Rogers had just tracked mud into the house. "Let me introduce you to someone," I heard, and then Rogers was on the phone. I saw this for the opportunity it was and decided to make hay.

We talked about how a man who has written less than five songs in his life has become such a universal touchstone. "He's the link," said Rogers. "He was really the last guy to hit the road with Woody, and he had such strong connections in Europe, where the Rod Stewarts and the Mick Jaggers saw him in English folk clubs and he turned them on to American roots music.

"He's not well-known to the general populace, and they don't understand how he knows all these people, or why they know him, but that's the way things have gone in our cultural context. There's all this division into musical camps. People don't understand . . . Jimmie Rodgers was a *pop* artist in his day. I asked Howlin' Wolf once, 'where'd you get that yodel?' 'I listened to Jimmie Rodgers on the radio comin' outta Nashville,' he said.

"Not to get too scholastic, but when we chose the songs for this album, we wanted them to be representative of Jack's whole context." The context is there, not only in the songs, and the singers, but in the sound of the album. Listen to Ramblin' Jack singing Townes Van Zandt's "Rex's Blues," and you hear Townes. Of course, listen to Townes, and you hear Jack. And while I may be trying too hard, when I heard Jack's high harmony behind Tom Waits on "Louise," my first thought was of Sara Carter. When he joins up with Jerry Jeff Walker on "Hard Travelin'" and "He Was a Friend of Mine," you're hearing music written by Woody Guthrie and Bob Dylan, but you're also hearing how Ramblin' Jack informed country's outlaw movement. His take on Joe Ely's "Me and Billy the Kid," plants him in the midst of the Austin scene. And so on, right through pop rock (for those of us introduced to Tim Hardin's "Reason to Believe" via Rod Stewart), Nashville, and Deadhead land.

"It's just him, covering a lot of different territory in American music," said Rogers. "But we didn't set out to make a nostalgic record. He's not a historical guy, he's right here now." And for the record, for all its musical cross-references, the album doesn't come off as a look-back. Even "Bleeker Street," a recent, rare Elliott composition, is set firmly in the present. The history is there, the whole Woody/Jack/Bob thing, but in the end, the song is about context. The here and now, how we got here, how it looks, and what we yet dare wish for.

Landlocked in dark Minneapolis, fitsing-and-startsing through the wet stoplights, Jack is telling the driver sea stories. He's tiny in the front seat, all hunched shoulders and hat. The salt-spray hiss of the tires plays beneath the narration.

". . . He went out the yardarm, on the foot-rope. The halyard parted. The yard crushed him. *By Way of Cape Horn*, that's the name of the book," he says. "You should read it. It's in the 917.8s."

He'll talk about trucks. He'll talk about ships. He'll talk about the Dewey Decimal System, for crying out loud. But Jack . . . what about the music? What'll I tell people?

"Tell'em my teeth are fallin' out, I can barely walk, and they better hurry up if they wanna see me, 'cuz I may not be around much longer." He's chuckling.

"But if I make it through this year, I'm gonna get me that 1947 Peterbilt and put another Cummins 220 in it, it's got a five and four, a long wheel base, I'm gonna put an old airstream trailer on the back of it, and man, we won't have to get on no god-damn airports *any*-more!"

I giggle. It's right there on the tape, completely unprofessional. But it gives Jack time to circle back along the yarn and come up with an answer.

"Tell'em I'm 19." ◄

► Anatomy of an Interview

I have long admired the work of musician Jay Farrar. Still, when the good folks at No Depression *assigned me the task of profiling the man, I knew I was being sent through daunting territory. "He speaks in haiku," warned one of the many writers previous who had tried and failed to elicit substantive comment from the songwriter. So, I decided to try something a little out of the ordinary. You can judge the results for yourself, although you may be interested in the thoughts of Zed from Alabama, whose subsequent letter to the magazine stated in part that, "I was appalled that you let a shmuck like Michael Perry interview Jay Farrar!" The letters were still coming six months later, culminating in a benchmark of sorts when Christopher from Canada deemed the piece "the worst interview in history." I believe it best to let Jorge Luis Borges respond on my behalf:*

Any time something is written against me, I not only share the sentiment but feel I could do the job far better myself. Perhaps I should advise would-be enemies to send me their grievances beforehand, with full assurance that they will receive my every aid and support. I have even secretly longed to write, under a pen name, a merciless tirade against myself.

Zed's complaints do not go unheard. I have taken to introducing myself at certain speaking engagements by having his letter read aloud.

A quick tip of the seed corn cap here to Grant Alden and Peter Blackstock, the co-editors of No Depression, *two fellers who not only allowed me to stumble into this trouble, but backed me when it came.*

No person can ever fully comprehend another, nor can any history be truly complete. Yet with practice, guidance, and self-awareness, you can learn to talk with a patient and obtain the comprehensive, organized set of data that constitutes the traditional health history. You must know (1) what information to get and (2) how to get it, while building a relationship as you proceed.

— Barbara Bates and Robert A. Hoekelman
from A Guide to Physical Examination *(Third Edition)*

When a nurse and patient convene to gather the patient's health

history, they enter into an implicit contract. The patient agrees to trust and confide in the nurse, and the nurse attempts to gather the information necessary to form a tentative diagnosis. Music journalism is not so different. By agreeing to be interviewed, the musician implies that he or she will trust and confide in the journalist; and the journalist attempts to gather the information necessary to support an explication of the artist.

Admittedly, beyond this point, the metaphor begins to show signs of strain. While it is in the patient's best interest to be forthright (assuming an accurate diagnosis is the first step toward a cure), the musician's motivations may be more complex, and unlike the nurse, even the kindest journalist is in no way ethically bound to operate in the best interests of the artist. Furthermore, perfectly healthy patients are rarely forced to subject themselves to in-depth prodding. Nor are their exam results made public. So, when one considers a publicity-shy musician faced with a journalist who essentially asks him to turn his head and cough — on the record — the metaphor is twisted out of shape.

Nonetheless, in preparing to interview the famously close-mouthed Jay Farrar about Son Volt's latest album, *Wide Swing Tremolo*, I couldn't help but think my former profession would come in handy. I recalled my days as a student nurse, when I diligently rehearsed my patient history gathering skills: Identifying Data, Chief Complaints, Present Illness, Past Medical History, Family History, Psychosocial History, right on down to Endocrinologic Maladies. I learned to facilitate, reflect, and clarify. I mastered the art of the empathic response. By the time I passed my boards, I could slap you into a backless gown and review your Twenty Systems before your buns chilled. Put me in a small room with a complete stranger, and within five minutes I'd have him cheerfully holding forth on everything from bowel habits to paroxysmal nocturnal dyspnea.

And yet, here I was on the phone with Jay Farrar and my

carefully arranged list of questions, and I was making a complete muckup of the whole thing, stammering and yammering, and losing my way.

Oh, for an exam room and a cold stethoscope.

You must modify your interviewing style according to the needs of the patient as they unfold.

— Bates and Hoekelman

Let's establish something: Jay Farrar isn't "difficult." He may be emotionally reclusive, but he seems to come by it honestly. He is not, in other words, *reclusive* in the way Michael Jackson is *reclusive*. He tolerates the interview process patiently. There are no derisive snorts or outbursts. But it's pretty clear he'd prefer to be just about anywhere but in that chair. A new album brings a new round of interviews, however, and *Wide Swing Tremolo* will raise a few questions. From the compressed, distorted vocals of the opening "Straightface," to "Jodel," a 38-second harmonica haunt, there is change afoot. The sound is unmistakably Son Volt, but where previous albums seemed linear, and tied to movement across the landscape, *Wide Swing Tremolo* is more about traveling without moving, in a landscape more emotional than geographical. Songs like the bagpipey instrumental "Chanty," and "Carry You Down," with its intermittent funereal drumstrokes, hovering flute, and spare piano accents evoke places envisioned rather than places seen.

Whatever the public reaction may be to these shifts, Farrar's talent and dedication to craft are already widely recognized. His music speaks for itself, and he seems resolutely determined that it remain so. And why not? And what does it say for the rest of us, that we aren't simply satisfied with what comes out of the speakers? That here we have an artist who doesn't want to crawl in the frame and crowd his own art, and yet we insist on dragging him out for close-ups?

So here was my first big idea: I'd do a profile packed with irre-futably detailed, way-inside, never-before-told tidbits about Jay Farrar the Mystery Music Man, with one little catch: None of it would be true. A complete fabrication, a character send-up cre-ated to match the mystery. Something along the lines of:

Jay Farrar has a pair of canary yellow patent leather Hush Puppies. "Them's my gardening shoes," he mumbles, as we pass through the breezeway on our way to play darts in the den. He seems oddly detached about the shoes, especially in light of the way their visual presence dominates the breezeway, a dim pas-sage framed in pale aluminum screens and gray cement paint.

He does pause, however, to point out his prize-winning beet. He hefts the beet, and for just the fraction of an instant, I see something deeper, a flicker of repressed joy, a wink from the Sphinx. I scribble a note about the beet, and resolve to return later and weigh it. When I look up, Farrar is gone, the beet abandoned.

The result? Nothing less than classic Socratic irony: "Behold your behind-the-scene tid-bits. Does their specious nature render them any less interesting? Do they make *Wide Swing Tremolo* any more or less interesting?" But when the perspicacious editors of this publication pointed out that Socratic irony might be distrib-uted via press clippings and interpreted as fact by journalists, I had visions of Son Volt being greeted at each gig with a fusillade of canned beets, a bruised Farrar finally forced to cancel the tour, hunt me down, and beat me senseless with a clunky yellow shoe.

I decided I'd just come up with some questions for the man.

The interview is initiated with those topics that are the least threatening to the patient and easiest to discuss.

— Jane Steinman Kaufman,
Medical-Surgical Nursing *(Second Edition)*

No Depression magazine: You've said that you thought of [previous albums] *Trace* and *Straightaways* as companion pieces. Does *Wide Swing Tremolo* fit within that context?

FARRAR: I don't think of it as a trilogy or anything like that. A lot of the songs were written for the previous two recordings during periods where we were on the road a lot. This one, most of the songs were either written in a period off the road, or written in periods of time where we were in the studio, because we spent more time in the studio this time than we had in the past. We spent eight weeks this time. The other [albums] were about half that. The songs on the previous recordings were written on the road; these songs were written in a period when the band was not on the road.

ND: Did that have an effect?

FARRAR: Yeah, I think so, I think with the previous recordings, there was a tendency to kind of write songs that would translate well to the live setting. On the one hand, that was exactly what I wanted to do with *Straightaways*, but I guess with this one, there were instances of writing songs from having picked up an instrument that was lying around, like a dulcimer or starting off writing a song on electric piano, which I hadn't done before.

ND: What impact did the new studio have? [*Wide Swing Tremolo* was recorded in Son Volt's warehouse rehearsal space near St. Louis.]

FARRAR: It's a different environment. I think it's an environment that's hard to beat as far as just being comfortable and finding inspiration, because it's an environment where you're used to finding inspiration during rehearsals.

ND: Is it easier to capture, since you're right there?

FARRAR: I think so, yeah. I was more concerned about trying to get good performance this time around than being worried about any kind of sonic purity.

ND: I read the article in *Musician* magazine that detailed the studio, right down to the model numbers of the cymbals hanging on the wall. What does that kind of article tell people?

FARRAR: [laughs, pauses] Ahhh . . . [deep breath] I really don't know. I think the guy just had fun putting little numbers on the dots.

ND: Does it provide valuable context to your music?

FARRAR: I wouldn't know.

As your knowledge and experience grow, you will limit your questions in some areas and expand them in others . . .

— Bates and Hoekelman

ND: Let me ask you this: Do you cook?

FARRAR: Do I cook?

ND: Yeah.

FARRAR: Ahh . . . yes, I do, sometimes.

ND: Okay. Well, if you cook a good meal for someone, will they think the meal tastes better if they know how your kitchen is set up?

FARRAR: Ahh . . . probably not. But maybe music and cooking are two different . . . ahh . . . activities completely

ND: In a sense it's a disingenuous question, but I am fascinated by someone saying, 'I love that music but that's not enough. I want to know what kind of strings they were using, I want to know where they were sitting when they recorded it, or I want to know more about the artist.' I'm always a little bit confused by that.

FARRAR: Actually, things like you mentioned do play a part, it's just a matter of how far you want to take it. I mean, certainly placement in a room has a lot to do with the ultimate sound, and strings can have an effect. Especially if it's the difference between flat wound strings or round wound strings. In a couple instances, on songs that had alternate tunings, a song like "Question," or something, I had to use really heavy gauge strings. Sometimes getting into detail is informative, and it matters.

Understand the client's perceptions of self and others.

— *Kaufman*

ND: Would you classify yourself as someone who's shy?

FARRAR: I don't know. I tend to shy away from psychoanalytical questions like that. [laughs]

ND: Someone told me you were 'painfully shy.' The question I would ask you is, if one is painfully shy, where does it hurt?

FARRAR: I . . . I . . . I don't accept the characterization.

ND: Someone else explained your reticence by telling me you were "strongly Midwestern," with "Midwestern inhibitions." As if Liberace had never happened. How would you define the demeanor of the "strongly Midwestern" man?

FARRAR: Ahh . . . I don't know. Where are you from?

ND: I'm from Wisconsin.

FARRAR: Where's Liberace from?

ND: Milwaukee.

FARRAR: Well, I guess, find Liberace, and we'll talk about it, and come to some sort of conclusion.

When I was a nurse, I had express permission and a responsibility to ask personal questions. The patient and I may have found the history-taking process uncomfortable, but we took some comfort from the thought that necessary work was being done. On the phone with Farrar, neither of us is so sure. And we're both too polite, too "strongly Midwestern" to make any definitive move. It doesn't come through in the transcript, but we're performing an elaborate, tentative courtesy dance amidst a swirl of ahs, ers, ums, and uncomfortable chuckles. He's embarrassed by the questions, and I'm embarrassed to be pressing him. It's not so much that I feel a wall between us, as a vacuum. He doesn't want to be characterized. He doesn't want to offend. You can hear all this in his voice.

ND: Is the stage, and the presentation of characters through song actually a fine way to hide right out in the wide open?

FARRAR: Possibly. It's certainly one way you can convey feelings . . . that maybe you couldn't, say, in a verbal sense. Putting it to song.

ND: I certainly don't see — and I apologize for using the word shy again, but I don't see that there's necessarily a contradiction between a performer and someone who's shy, because you're presenting your art more than yourself. Of course there's the whole argument about whether you can separate those or not.

FARRAR: Yes. I think it's irrelevant, personally.

ND: Do you see your songs as fiction or nonfiction?

FARRAR: Ahh . . . I guess it's mixed, y'know. It depends on the song. I was never taught how to write songs, so I generally don't write narrative-type songs or songs that tell stories. I do sometimes, but in general the songs are probably more just a lyrical collage. Or impressions.

ND: Is that how they unfold? Obviously not in some ABAB format. Do they come to you lyrically or sonically?

FARRAR: Generally the music is written first. I mean, I write lyrics separately too, but generally I put the lyrics to the song. But it happens all different ways for me. I've never really settled into a method of writing. It can happen all ways.

Assist the client to identify needs, conflicts, or problems.

— Kaufman

ND: My original concept for this article was to make everything up. [I explain about the shoes and the beets.]

FARRAR: [chuckles] That's an interesting approach! I would tend to agree with what you're saying, but it's understandable why people want to know more.

ND: Are they looking for context?

FARRAR: Yeah . . . Like I said before, I completely understand why people would want to know how things were recorded, as opposed to whether or not the person is shy, or what relevance that has to the way the songs were written, or the final version, the way it sounds.

ND: Would your life be easier if writers just made things up and left you alone?

FARRAR: [laughs] Probably.

ND: [flailing] Do you ever just sing carefree songs?

FARRAR: [laughs]

ND: For example — keeping in mind that I live in a tiny town of 485 people, and I'm a single guy living in my house — I used to love to sing along to Donna Fargo's "The Happiest Girl in the Whole U.S.A." while I was dusting, until one day I got caught by the town maintenance man. He'd been knocking on the door for two minutes and I hadn't noticed him. Do you ever just sing your heart out?

FARRAR: Ahh . . . sing absurd songs?

ND: [hopefully] Sure!

FARRAR: I guess not too often. Certainly melodies can get inside your head that you don't particularly want there.

ND: Are you familiar with any of George Thorogood's work?

FARRAR: Only in a peripheral way, from what I've heard on the radio. I don't own any of it.

ND: What do you think of that song of his, "You Talk Too Much"?

FARRAR: Ahh . . . I'm not familiar with that one.

Before leaving the patient the nurse should summarize the major ideas offered by the patient and inform him or her when contact will be made.
                                                            — *Kaufman*

Sounds like things are going well, Jay. *Wide Swing Tremolo* is unmistakably Son Volt, but it's got a more experimental feel. It's a

bit more sonically exploratory, a little less organic. I hear you saying that you prefer to offer your music over your personality, and I
empathize with that. I won't be contacting you anytime soon.
Maybe, just out of guilt for putting you through this, I'll send you
a nice piece of pie. It would be the Midwestern thing to do.

> *Skilled clinicians may demonstrate a disconcerting ability to ask the one addi-*
> *tional question that unlocks the door to understanding and to do so in a tenth*
> *of the time you have spent. Let this be a stimulus rather than a discouragement!*
> — Bates and Hoekelman

Maybe next time. ◄

▶ Insoluble Toxins

There were supposed to be chicken livers. This, I was told, was how the rough bunch reconstituted themselves all those mornings ago when Mike Magnuson was a loud-drinking music school dropout working the production line at Jennico, pouring plastic, writing a radio play a week, joining friends to watch the sun rise through the raised butt of a beer bottle. Morning was a hazy, red-rimmed business, and the raggle-taggle group would decamp to Chicken Hut, to brace their blood with the ferric tang of chicken livers. A horde of hangovers were appeased at the Chicken Hut, where the air was so strung with second-hand smoke, and the windows so grease-glazed that the place itself seemed permanently hung over. Now Magnuson was on a national book tour, and would squeeze in an unscheduled reading at the college where he had finally graduated with an English degree in 1989. Friends and teachers remained from the salad days, and there were predictions of a raging evening and a chicken liver morning. I had heard chicken liver stories again and again. I visualized the petite brown organs in deep-fried heaps, the breading aglisten with grease, ready to be speared with an overturned fork, swabbed in ketchup, and consumed to the tune of robust banter. This would be a loud-mouthed, lubricious feast: A writer was returning home, on tour and hardbound.

The Right Man For The Job (HarperCollins) is Mike Magnuson's first novel. It is the tale of Gunnar Lund, a self-loathing but oddly hopeful man who repossesses chintzy living room sets for a rental agency in the desperate sectors of Columbus, Ohio. Gunnar describes himself as Scandinavian, six feet tall, pale and thick about the abdomen, with a torso like raised bread dough. In

Wisconsin he was a state university music major, but he couldn't make it stick. Ended up putting in eight years as a "wrench" at a plastics factory, where his days were "ten hours of grease and sweat, five hours drinking, and the rest either sleeping or driving to work or the bar." When Gunnar philanders his way into the arms of a lover who decides to attend graduate school at Ohio State, Gunnar follows, leaving wedding plans and a fiancée behind. "I migrated to Ohio for love," he says, but three months later, his steel-toed boots are still stuck with plastic dust, and the relationship is pustulant with recriminations and hate. Gunnar snatches brief moments of respite by sneaking out on his bicycle, his unlikely bulk stacked over the slim frame, ". . for a moment released . . . my soul made better from the road, my inner life built of my pumping legs and heavy lungs. . . ." In the end, he cannot ride long enough. "I am guilty of much in this life . . . I am a leaver of brides at the altar, or a bride. . . . I am guilty of jilting."

"I guess I'm not a good man."

This is Gunnar Lund. And this is also Michael Magnuson.

Eau Claire, Wisconsin, was a sawmill town born at the confluence of the Chippewa and Eau Claire rivers. When lumbering died, and automobiles replaced horses, the gigantic Uniroyal tire plant gave a blue-collar man something to turn his hand to. Then, in the mid- to late 1980s, the plant shut down. It was about this time that Mike Magnuson was churning out detergent bottles for Jennico, a small company occupying a tin building at the weedy north edge of town. It was work that strengthened the back and drained the soul, and he was glad to have it. These days, Jennico has been taken over by a larger corporation, the Uniroyal plant has been remodeled into offices, craft stores and dance studios, and a relentless mall sprawl south of town has left the job market deceptively swollen with positions in part-time retail — just the thing for University of Wisconsin–Eau Claire students marking

time between keggers and visits from the folks. Somehow, you figure *The Right Man For The Job* might never have happened if
Michael Magnuson had sailed through music school while folding
shirts at The Gap.

By his own estimation, Magnuson has held "thirty-five, forty
jobs," nearly all of them short-term, and nearly all of them obtained on the strength of his back. He has mowed lawns, mixed
concrete, blacktopped driveways, run jackhammers, driven a laundry van, worked as a janitor. For his dust-jacket photograph,
Magnuson was posed in a vaguely industrial setting, wearing a
sleeveless black t-shirt. His bangs were moistened at the fringe.
You can see what was intended, but the image is antiseptic. I ask
Magnuson how much of the novel's promotion involved prostitu-
tion of his "factory guy" image. "They did do that," he says. "And
it's as much my fault as anything else. Because I'm proud of having had those jobs, and I don't have anything else I can talk about.
But that angle didn't project me into the Oprah Winfrey book club
or anything. The fact is, I don't think anybody gives a shit about
working class folk. I'm certain that a person like me who doesn't
write "popular fiction" — no doctors, lawyers, movie stars — when
it comes to my third book I may need to look for a new publisher,
or not publish at all. It's such a market-driven business. I don't see
that I'll have a book a year and become one of the great figures of
American literature. I meet writers all the time who think that
way, but I don't . . . I'm not writing enduring classics. I'm just
trying to do the best I can to avoid going back to the factory.

"The sleeveless shirt, standing in front of the machinery — it's
true, sort of, but it could never be what it really is. What real
factory people are like, the things that make them laugh, I really
couldn't publish those things. I couldn't use the language, be as
graphic." In other words, the working class requires a shave and
haircut (and a clean sleeveless t-shirt) before it can be champi-
oned. That said, while *The Right Man for the Job* harpoons

academia and privilege, it is free of the disingenuous romanticization of hard work or the people who perform it. Magnuson knows there is no especial honor or dishonor in hard work, nor is it redemptive — for all his labor, Gunnar Lund is hardly the stuff of makeover "after" pictures. He is a weak-willed bundle of contradictions; simultaneously his own harshest critic and self-indulgent stooge. In other words, a perfect medium of truth.

It was cold the night Mike Magnuson returned to Eau Claire, but then it was March in Wisconsin, and snow would fall through May. Representatives of NOTA, the campus literary arts organization for which he had once served as editor, took Magnuson to dinner. His light ginger hair was trimmed, as was his mustache. His cloth pants and light shirt were worlds removed from the factory. A fresh generation of students sat to his left, silent and regarding him the way one might a large uncultured relative of whom they had heretofore only heard stories. Magnuson's former Jennico co-worker, drinking partner and writing workshop foil, Frank Smoot, sat to his right. Bruce Taylor, the professor who first singled out Magnuson and bullied him into writing, sat two tables away. In his first workshop, Taylor told Magnuson he had talent, but that he needed ten years' work before he'd be publishable. Magnuson responded by threatening Taylor with physical assault. "When you see people with that kind of talent," Taylor says today, "you know you have to lean on them harder. He was better than the others, but not that much better." Magnuson dropped out of school to work in the factory, but Taylor would still look at his writing, feed him dinner, put him up on his couch. In the end, says Taylor, "he went from being talented to being a writer." Taylor claims he saw *The Right Man for the Job* through four drafts. Nursing a whiskey, chain-smoking Carltons and looking like a father whose son has returned from the front with a wound and decorations, he told me, "I just want to watch this."

The reading is held in a curtained-off section of the university ballroom, which, apart from a parquetry floor, is blandly institutional. Backed by a pale brown floor-to-ceiling drape, Magnuson reads from behind a boxy rostrum. His reading voice is pitched higher than you'd expect from a man so bulky and tall. His tone possesses a plaintive earnestness; his delivery reflects a musician's sensitivity to rhythm. And here were the surest signs that this was a Wisconsin writer: His flat, extended a's, lingering t's, his hard r's so much like our own. We cling to our r's, bend them all the way over, wear them out. His d's, too, had a familiar thud, dropping like a five-pound weight into a feather pillow — and we have more d's than most, as our th's are frequently converted to d's.

The first selection is a short story set in a nursing home. The narrator is a piano playing nurse's aide who writes a fugue to win the attention of a woman. The piece is written in the form of a fugue, with the same cadences and repetitions of theme. Magnuson wrote it to impress the woman who is now his wife.

He switches to selections from the novel. He is perspiring like a laborer. Setting up his final piece, he swabs his brow and references his HarperCollins handlers: "They told me never to read this scene." He flips his two middle fingers toward an imaginary balcony of public relations advisors. "But I'm home. Fuck'em." The piece — in which the main character in *The Right Man For The Job* brains a customer's dog — builds slowly, stratifying and gaining momentum, resolves with a crunching abruptness, then dissipates in a soft coda. Magnuson finishes, and there is that moment when a writer is trapped at the podium, the audience still silent, unsure that the thing is over. He replaces his glasses, retreats from the podium and mops his neck. Bruce Taylor hands him an inscribed toilet plunger — a gag award commemorating an overtly scatological bit of juvenilia Magnuson performed at a reading in the early days — and announces that "Books are available in the back, and Mike will stay here forever to sign them."

Back in the days when Magnuson was in and out of school, molding plastic and writing for no other purpose than to put the necessary mileage on his keyboard, he did much of his drinking and boasting in a narrow tavern called The Joynt. Proprietor Bill Nolte once edited Donald Hall's *To Read Poetry*, and the walls are lined with poster-sized black-and-white prints of folk, jazz, and blues legends who have played the tiny room. Just inside the door, tucked to the right, a small table has served as the unofficial center of the Eau Claire literary scene for years. John Ciardi, Gary Snyder, Miller Williams, Donald Hall, and Seamus Heaney have all slid their knees beneath the table in "poet's corner." It was simply natural that Magnuson return to this spot, and when the last book was signed, he did.

In the beginning, it was like the old days: Fat and loud, bluff and boisterous. The clink and tunk of beer glasses on wood. A scrap of conversation: "I'd be willing to sell you the negatives . . ." Magnuson's voice: ". . . and I can't go in the Wal-Mart gun shop anymore." Magnuson and Taylor trade the role of raconteur between them, burning an endless rope of Marlboros and Carltons. Magnuson smokes with distracted disregard, switching cigarettes from hand to hand, wedging them indiscriminately between any combination of digits. When the cigarette finally does land in his mouth, the impression is that it has been placed there only to free the hands for gesticulation.

But the old stories are quickly told, and the bombast loses steam just as quickly. The crowd is thin. Taylor leaves early. In truth, the "scene" in general at the Joynt has declined in recent years. The big names no longer show, the regulars are of a new generation. Magnuson and Smoot carry on, but their tone is subdued, seasoned. Like so many friends linked by the past, they have found the present irrelevant.

On my way out of town, I drop Magnuson at his hotel. The last image I have of him that evening: He is walking to the lobby doors, dangling a plastic bag embossed with the university logo: "Excellence." A wooden toilet plunger protrudes from the bag. Still digging for his room key, Magnuson walks through the doors of the Hampton Inn. It is not yet midnight.

Magnuson, Smoot, and Taylor have agreed to meet me in the morning at Chicken Hut — now known as Randy's, but still open 24 hours, and still serving chicken livers. At 11 a.m., the trio still hasn't shown. Eventually, I locate Smoot and Magnuson at a local coffee shop. As it turns out, smoking is now prohibited at Randy's. And so the three men have been at a local Perkins outlet, where the windows sparkle and the menus are upbeat and grease-free, but the burning of nicotine is still tolerated on one side of a frosted glass partition. Chicken livers are not available. To compensate, Magnuson offers to take me for a drive through the Eau Claire he remembers. Frank Smoot joins us.

Magnuson drives a rental car along the route he used to take to his job in a plastics factory. In the old days, it was always a bike. "Six miles, every day," he says. We pass a local high school. Magnuson slaps the wheel, launches into a story. "During the 1988 presidential campaign, George Bush was up here and he was gonna take the road to the airport, which is right ahead. I was biking past, and it was right about the time school got out. I regularly got shit from high school students on this road, so when I hear behind me, `Pull off the road!' I go, `Fuuuck you,' and whip the bird, and by God, this car nosed in front of me and I had to jump the curb, and I wiped out. Secret Service dudes jumped out, and they examined me, looked at my bike pump and stuff, because Bush was just about to come down the road. Well, Christ, I didn't know!" He laughs. "That's one of the reasons I hate that fucker." It's a funny story, but when he tells it, you can hear the voice of the proletariat, sneering from the mud as the king rolls past.

We reach the site where the old Jennico was located. Operations have been moved up the road to a capacious steel structure. The building in which Smoot and Magnuson worked sits empty, the blue tin faded and saggy. "This is it," says Magnuson. "Looks like it's . . ." He searches for the word, then settles on a favorite. " . . . *fucked*."

He peers around. "Yeah, it's all gone. There used to be big hoppers full of plastic. We were making plastic bottles for detergents. It was an extrusion blow-molding operation." He gestures at the surroundings, a soulless landscape of distribution centers and loading docks, most surrounded by chain link fence. "There wasn't all this shit . . . this was all field when we worked here. We'd go out back to smoke dope at four in the morning and pretend there were giraffes comin' out of it — 'see the giraffe, dude?' It was Africa!"

Magnuson swears half of the old factory was knowingly built over an illegal toxic waste dump. He's also convinced that a massive chemical spill that occurred during his tenure was an insurance ruse. "I was pretty open-mouthed about it, and was always in trouble. I'd tell anybody anything. That was one of my big problems here.

"Plus, I would correct the punctuation on the memos and shit. Oh, ho, ho, they hated my guts." This is a common Magnuson trait; a coda of humor after the bad news. *The Right Man for the Job* is similarly arranged; for a man describing "the dirge and constant look back that has become my life," Gunnar Lund says a lot of funny things. His story is deeply sad, but it is not drab.

We drive away from the factory. Magnuson is looking for a place called Slim's Saddle Bar. We find it just up the road, the lot full at 11:30 a.m. "We'd get off at seven in the morning and come up here," says Magnuson. "They didn't have stools — you sat on saddles. I remember sitting here for seven hours and leaving with a saddle sore." We drive on, past Hobbsy's, another working class bar notorious for production line drinking and vicious fights. Magnuson did his share of drinking, but he wouldn't fight. "I just don't believe in that kinda shit. I mean, in theory, I like the idea of kickin' the shit out of somebody, but I never have done it, and I never will. It's true. I never have hit anybody in the face in my whole life.

"Most nights, I'd ride home drunk, or I'd stay at somebody's trailer." He gestures at the trailer parks near the industrial park. "We'd drink in the bar, then we'd drink in the trailer, and I'd bike home at 5 in the morning, and then we'd go to the Beehive at 5:30 in the morning and have ourselves some Bloody Marys." He pauses. "I feel bad it all happened. I really do. I'm not prone to fuckin' around much anymore. If I would have applied myself, maybe things would have been a lot different."

But he did apply himself. And he didn't drink every night. Frank Smoot remembers Magnuson writing four or five hours a day during the factory years. Furthermore, I suggest that the novel suggests these experiences were an artistic necessity. Magnuson ponders, then muses, "Yeah, I can see that's the logical thing to think . . . but I really wish it wouldn't have happened. I don't really give a shit that I have something to write about." I point out that this could be perceived as disingenuous, considering the rich source material he has to work with, and how he has leveraged it into book contracts, graduate school, a professorship. "No, I mean that. I should be grateful for the subject matter, but you know, I don't think it's 'fun' to the down-and-out folk. It was the bad old days . . . I'd drink, cheat on my old lady one terrible thing after another."

I hear the sound of Gunnar's shame in Magnuson's voice. Shame is most powerful when we earn it. But shame is also a powerful tool of truth. When you have failed your own soul, or worse yet, failed at the expense of someone else's soul, you are vested with a weary authority; with the ability to say *do not do what I have done, it will ruin you.* The important lessons we always learn one remove too late, and Gunnar's truth is a weary and regretful truth. It does little to edify him, but it gives him moral authority a finger-wagging preacher can only pretend to. Gunnar no longer has the strength or sense of self-worth to speak in code, or tell hopeful lies. If you find his truth unpalatable, or revolting, or disturbing, he no longer cares. He is a man enervated by regret, driven from disaster to disaster only by a desperate desire to atone — all the while certain he will fail in the attempt. Magnuson again: "Even though I'm starting to get a more comfortable life, I got this weight, man, I am convinced that I am a bad man. That even if I try to do something good it's not really good, that I'm doing it for a reason, that I'm trying to fuck with people who'll give me something.

"I would have rather been a good Christian young man."

In nursing school, I gained the impression that the liver stockpiled insoluble toxins. I have always assumed that to ingest liver is to ingest all the insoluble toxins the former owner of said organ ingested over its lifetime. Thus, though I like the taste, I have always avoided consuming this organ. Nonetheless, for the purpose of this story, I was determined to experience the chicken liver rite firsthand. And so, with Magnuson gone on his way to Minneapolis, I sat down at Randy's and had a low-key, smoke-free plate of deep-fried chicken livers. Lightly breaded and brown on the outside, they were mealy and yellow on the inside, and after each swallow a trace metal aftertaste remained. Magnuson's old friend Frank Smoot joined me, and we talked about how things once were, and how they were now, and we cast about for ways to say you can never go home again without saying you can never go home again. Failing, we concentrated on the chicken livers, going heavy on the ketchup. Then we went our separate ways.

Nothing meets the measure of memory. There was no triumphal homecoming; it was an idea none of the players involved should have been susceptible to in the first place. In *The Right Man For The Job*, Gunnar Lund wonders if his persistent recollections of Wisconsin, "where the talk is of deer hunting and the fate of the Green Bay Packers. . . . I remember clipped lawns and pine trees and lilac hedges. . . . Wisconsin life, you know, is simple as a goddam spoon," are fabricated memories. For a moment he tries to sort truth from legend. Then he says simply, "Our lives are better remembered as lies." ◄

▶ The Road Ahead:
Life of the American Trucker

John Steinbeck was a student of truckers. One need only read the second chapter of *The Grapes of Wrath* to know this. A trucker gives Tom Joad a lift, and Steinbeck's economical, precisely-drawn portrait of the man — a minor character, after all — reveals his depth of understanding of the profession and its rhythms. Twenty years later, Steinbeck bought a pickup truck and returned to the roads of America with his dog, Charley. It was 1960, and the first generation of travel centers had been spawned by the Interstate Highway Act of 1956. When he required gasoline, Steinbeck would circle to the rear of the complex, where the big trucks fueled. As the journey unfolded, he reacquainted himself with truck drivers. *Travels with Charley*, the book that followed, contained the following passage:

> They are a breed set apart from the life around them, the long-distance truckers—They are clannish and they stick together, speaking a specialized language — By listening to them talk I accumulated a vocabulary of the road. . . .

The vocabulary of the road draws deeply from a lexicon of tempo and flow. The trucker's muse is Independence, but in a livelihood fueled by commerce and sustained through motion, the muse is constantly dogged by twin taskmasters: Time and Distance. Time is marked by mileposts, distance is furled into the odometer, but neither can be corralled. The trucker is constantly closing in on a destination, but the pursuit is Sisyphean; when the load arrives, the destination changes.

In general, it is a good time to be a trucker. Driver pay has been steadily rising. Industry publications are thick with advertisements placed by shippers desperate for drivers. At the gigantic Mid-America Trucking Show in Louisville last March, roughly 140 booths were dedicated to driver recruitment. While there is some debate about whether or not a true driver shortage exists, everyone agrees on one thing: Job turnover is occurring at an unprecedented rate. For a disgruntled trucker a fresh start is just a phone call away.

Because it's a driver's market, trucking companies go to great lengths to get drivers in their trucks and keep them there. Incentives range from tailored pay and benefit plans to cash advances. Some insure family members at no extra cost so they may ride as passengers. Cardinal Freight Carriers sends its top drivers on free vacations. Schneider National, based in Green Bay, Wisconsin, gave six of its top drivers new pick-up trucks in 1998; they also sponsored NASCAR driver Dick Trickle, who raced across national TV in a Schneider-orange Monte Carlo with the company's 1-800 recruitment number plastered across its hood. An ad for the TransAm trucking company in *Road King* magazine promises drivers specially appointed sleeper cabs, satellite access, and "easy" bonus pay. They also promise "95 percent No Touch Freight," and "No New York City," meaning you'll rarely have to unload your own load, and you'll never have to do it after fighting New York City traffic.

It is revealing, however, that in an industry with a footloose reputation, the most universal and consistently touted perk is, quite simply: *home*. "Get Home Every Week," promises BJ Transport in *rpm* magazine. An ad for McElroy Truck Lines features a picture of a young boy with a baseball bat, under the heading, "You'll also be a hit this weekend at your child's T-ball game." To keep house and home together, the trucker must leave home. It is a paradoxical conundrum, summed up — intentionally or not — in the headline of an ad for All American Transport "Owner Operators and Drivers: Want Home Time??? Need Miles???"

You do need the miles. Miles are money. And so you climb into the cab and point the hood down the road. For all the open space out there, you'll often find the road a tight fit. For one thing, your truck is bigger than it has ever been. Standard trailer lengths run from 45 to 53 feet, and sometimes stretch to 57 feet. That trailer is wider and taller than ever also, at 102 inches by 110 inches. Loaded, you might weigh 80,000 pounds and take up 70 feet of road from bumper to back door. A passenger sedan traveling 55 miles per hour can stop in 133 feet; you will require 196 to 335 feet. All these things make your fellow travelers nervous. To make a right turn in tight quarters, you need to swing into the left lane, then cut off the right lane. You have blind spots off your front bumper that can hide a good-sized car; you have a blind spot to the rear that can hide a good-sized class of third graders. In order to get up to speed after sitting at a red light, you may have to work your way through ten or more gears. All these things make your fellow travelers irritable.

There are people who would like to see you off the road so they can drive unimpeded to the mall, where the shelves are filled with inexpensive goods. But truckers have a saying: If you bought it, a truck brought it. It's a simplistic slogan but tough to argue with. Our voracious, just-in-time materialism keeps the truckers running, puts them on the road as part of a consumer-driven dynamic in which we are all complicit.

If you took this job because you love the sound of rolling wheels, you also know that the average trucker spends 15 to 20 hours per week on nondriving activities. You are required to maintain a driver's log, accounting for your activities at 15-minute intervals around the clock. Time spent on paperwork is especially frustrating if you are paid by the mile. So is time spent maintaining your truck. *Commercial Carrier Journal* this year listed over 200 "out of service" standards — ranging from leaking brake fluid to damaged wiring — any one of which can be grounds for the government sidelining your rig during a roadside inspection. If you are stopped and subjected to a North American Standard Level III Driver-Only Inspection Procedure, you'll be expected to produce your driver's license, a medical examiner's certificate, records of duty status, driver's daily vehicle inspection report, documentation of periodic inspections, shipping papers and/or bills of lading, and receipts or other documents as requested. If you wear a hearing aid, the inspector can ask you to prove that you carry a spare power source.

You may have taken this job because you like the idea of independence, life on the open road. But more and more, you'll have someone riding with you, looking over your shoulder. Many companies now track their trucks with satellites, what the drivers call being "bird-dogged." It's tough to imagine yourself as an unfettered cowboy when a dispatcher in Albany can tell if you were speeding when you shot through Chouteau, Oklahoma, or if you stopped for that railroad crossing just outisde Des Moines, or how long you spent in the shower at your last fuel stop. In the dispatch center of Southern Pride Trucking of San Diego, a computerized wall map of the United States shows where the company's trucks are in real time. An advertisement for a satellite trucking firm in *Commercial Carrier Journal* boasts about a system that can monitor your truck engine for over-revving, idle speed and idle time. Never mind your truck, they're tracking your foot.

Of course all of these things — the paperwork, the inspections, the satellites — came about for a reason. Trucking companies and shippers remain competitive by trimming every wasted minute from the transport process. Government regulations such as drug-testing and much of the required paperwork are a response to safety issues. When the trucking industry deregulated in 1981, there was a concurrent upsurge in trucking-related accidents and fatalities. The deregulated market made more room for upstarts and renegades who compromised safety on the road.

However, according to *Sharing the Road*, a John Deere Transportation Insurance publication, accident-related deaths involving tractor-trailers have been in generally steady decline since 1985, even as the number of trucks and miles driven have soared. Post-deregulation fatalities peaked at 4,517 in 1985, when trucks traveled between 70 and 80 billion annual vehicle miles. By 1995, fatalities had fallen to 3,576 while annual vehicle miles had risen to 115 billion. The National Highway and Traffic Safety Administration reports that in 71 percent of truck related fatalities, the truck driver was not at fault.

Citizens for Reliable and Safe Highways (CRASH) doesn't feel things have improved sufficiently. Among other things, CRASH claims that "although big trucks are only 3 percent of all registered motor vehicles, big truck-passenger vehicle crashes annually account for more than one of every five motor vehicle deaths." It also claims the trucking industry's recent growth means "thousands of commercial truck drivers have been put behind the wheels of enormous, dangerous vehicles without the necessary skills even though they have successfully passed their state's Commercial Driving License (CDL) examination." It is true that simply passing a test does not prove one is a good driver. In fact, the road has its share of dangerous truck drivers. Shipping pressures contribute to driver fatigue — although recent fatigue studies have shown that even driver fatigue is not as simply understood as we once thought. Accidents — some horrific — are inevitable. But the vast preponderance of truck drivers are more skilled than anyone on the road, operating under private and government scrutiny that would send the average commuter screaming to his congressman.

If you're in search of true trucker *zeitgeist*, one of the more informative things you can do is buy a citizens band radio and tune it to Channel 19. That's where the truckers hang out, in a rolling coffee klatch. The truckers who talk on 19 reveal a lot about themselves, good and bad. The old-timers bemoan the amount of profanity and lewd subject matter that crops up, and truth be told, an hour's worth of listening in heavy traffic is not recommended for the easily offended. As in any public arena, the quiet, well-reasoned opinion is underrepresented, although frequently, when a driver gets especially profane, the heretofore silent voices start popping in, telling him to take it somewhere else, or to remember that the public may be listening. The loudmouth usually responds with an escalating flurry of epithets, but in a surprising number of cases, peer pressure triumphs, and the tirade fizzles.

On 19, truckers argue about horsepower and fuel mileage, miss their kids, and warn each other about "Smokey" and obstructions in the road ahead. They talk about home like sailors talk about shore leave. They complain about the road, the job, the pay, and sadistic dispatchers who never let them go home. If a woman's voice comes on the air, the truckers walk all over each other, jamming the frequency like a pack of wolves chasing a rabbit through a culvert. Eavesdropping on Channel 19 is an exercise in audio anthropology. You learn about the job, you learn about the road, and, by inference, you learn the lingo. On a recent trip to Louisville, I heard several truckers warning us southbounders that there was a "gator in the hammer lane." Near as I could tell, we were a bit too far north for gators, but when I crested a hill and straddled a hulking chunk of rubber unfurled from somebody's retread, I understood.

You listen, and you learn about trucking and the life that goes with it. One sunny afternoon on a Wisconsin highway, two truckers are discussing whether it's better to be paid by weight, by percentage, or by the mile. "I gotta coast, or all my money goes up the exhaust pipe!" says the one hauling by the mile. "I been haulin' tankers since '64 . . . ," says the other driver who's got a shock of white hair. He's hooked to a load of petrol, placarded "FLAMMABLE," and the other driver has just passed him. "Hell, you seen my hair!"

Along the same stretch of highway, another voice: "Whatcha got there, northbound?"

"A load of dispatcher brains."

Northbound is running empty.

Another trucker, weary of burning precious fuel in a head wind, looks for a trailer to draft behind. "I need a door!"

Around the larger truckstops, you'll hear truckers offering pallets for sale, or tow straps. Fast-talking hucksters hawk CB equipment, urge you to come on up to Channel 40 for details. Female voices offer to clean cabs, wash windows, and provide a selection of other services.

Channel 19 isn't the place for longwinded chitchat. If you want to discuss the evolution of trucking as culture or last week's NASCAR results, courtesy dictates that you "meet" your fellow conversationalist at one of the other 38 available channels (Channel 9 is reserved for emergencies). A certain amount of self-policing occurs, not all of it polite, not all of it civil. Generally, the exchanges on Channel 19 are short, directly related to road conditions, vehicle positioning, or questions of orientation.

"Hey northbound, you OK?" It's snowing, and a rig in the opposite lane is pulled to the shoulder, hazard lights flashing.

"Blew out my front steer tire. I got help coming."

"OK, Bud, long as yer warm. See ya."

Another voice: "Looks like he sassed when he shoulda shayed!"

A Kenworth passes a Peterbilt. As soon as the Kenworth's trailer is clear of the Peterbilt's front bumper, the Peterbilt's driver is on the radio. "Got'er if y'want'er, K-Walker."

"I do appreciate it." The Kenworth pulls in.

The drivers make fun of each other and their rides. An International is an "Inter-trash-ional." A Cummins engine is a "Come-along."

And they talk about home. One trucker talks about his son, getting in trouble, drinking and not coming in at night. His conversation partner, a stranger, offers sympathy, then talks about the price his own family pays for his absence. "I'm watchin' my daughter grow up in pictures."

Often, especially in the darkness, you'll hear two drivers talking just to talk, stretching out a topic that was thin to begin with, extending it just to hear a voice along the miles.

For all their visibility on the highway, it is almost as if truckers exist in a parallel universe, separate but inextricably essential to our own. "It is a whole pattern of life," wrote Steinbeck, "little known to the settled people along the routes of the great trucks." He studied them, talked to them, rode beside them, and then, having described them as best he could, concluded, "I learned only enough about these men to be sure I would like to know much more." ◄

▶ Branding God

Throughout my childhood and young adulthood, "going to church" meant going to someone's home on Sunday morning and gathering quietly in the living room. We prayed, sang a few austere a cappella hymns and read verses from the Bible before offering up brief, homemade homilies. You could usually smell a roast simmering in the kitchen adjacent. There was deep comfort in the quiet assemblage.

When I was sixteen, I began a five-year stint working on a Wyoming ranch run by a family of my same religion. I didn't know it then, but I was taking the first steps on a skeptic's journey. Today, I can no longer believe as I once did. But I am no bitter heretic. The people in this story, the people I met with for an entire childhood of Sunday mornings, the parents who raised and taught me in love, are people whom, quite simply and profoundly, I owe.

Brother Tim Copper was preaching brimstone, and God Himself was bringing the backbeat. We were gathered in a long, empty, quonset-style granary, seated on wooden benches, receiving the Word. All around the granary, wheat fields stretched away for miles. Brother Tim was working Revelations, if my recollection is correct — and it might not be, I had my eye on this particular girl — and the Good Lord was working a towering thunder bank just off to the southwest, sliding it in on golden shafts of setting sun and legs of lightning, all the while staccato-dancing his fingers across a kettledrum forged in the storms of Jupiter. The hot wind pushed sweet rain-a-comin' dust under the granary door and set the ladies skirts to stirring. Bible pages riffled, and the young girls put their hands to their hair lest it come unpinned. Brother Tim had Revelations, he had the terrible, swift sword a-flashing from the sky, and he had the admonitory thunder. He had the groove.

I'll give him this: He knew how to work it. The nearer that

storm drew, the more the wind made the roofing nails squawk and the tin roof retch, the taller he rose, glowering from the plywood riser, squeezing the Word in one hand, index finger bookmarking verses he knew by rote. His perfervid eyes swept the congregation like a shark working a beach. This was no come to the warm and sheltering bosom of Christ speech, this was an operatic Armageddon rafter rattler. Brother Tim was recommending Heaven by pointing the way to Hell, double-timing our sorry souls like a drill instructor assigned a platoon of pudgy mollycoddles. The march was on, he said, lag behind and be damned. We trembled with truth.

We weren't used to this sort of thing. Our Sunday meetings were hushed, reverent affairs, parsed with *sotto voce* prayer, subdued testimony, and muted hymns. Even for this, the Saturday night service of our yearly convention, a service in which the meeting is typically "tested" at the conclusion to see if anyone will stand and silently profess their willingness to walk with God, the thunder from the dais was unexpected and unusual. Even I, distracted as I was by the young nursing student two rows forward and one bench down, found myself caught up in the terrible power of the whole thing, moved by the cinematics of it all: Brother Tim's bituminous eyes, his portentous certainty, the way he seemed to summon thunder each time he punched the air with his bible. It was as if Wagner's Valkyries had dropped in on the Quakers.

I don't go to church anymore. I was a young cowboy then, working summers on a ranch in Wyoming. Six days a week we worked, with Sunday a strictly observed day of rest. Sunday came from another world. We sat through meeting reverent in our clean socks and stiff boots, then lazed in the cool bunkhouses or fiddled around down by the river. Out by the shop, the equipment that smoked and roared all week sat silent. I used to stand among the tools on the cool concrete and look out through the greasy glass panes over the grinder and marvel at the way the ranch changed on its day off. A permeant placidity settled over everything, from the wood-chucks sunning on the junk piles to the tall grass waving easy on the plateau above the river. Today, an afternoon seems constrained, only a matter of hours. Then, on a Sunday, time was expansive, gracious, accommodating.

One Sunday, after meeting had drawn to a close and we had returned our bibles to our bunkhouses, we gathered in the cookhouse for dinner. I remember roast beef and gravy, but then that would be a fairly safe bet. The women had a little extra bustle about them this Sunday, because brother Tim Copper was at the table. In our little corner of Wyoming, Brother Tim was seen as the heavyweight champ of preaching. Church members would grin and shake their heads in benevolent wonder when recounting his exploits; the deeper implication was that he was not to be messed with. Preaching or not, Brother Tim tended to Hold Forth. This day he was in strong, confident voice, sharing the stories of sinners and their weakness in the face of salvation. There was a woman nearby who had been coming to church off and on for some time. She was a beautiful thing, and, as the story went, had worked as a model. We heard anecdotes of her struggle, of her inability to adhere to our dress code, for which women are forbidden to cut their hair or wear pants. After working with her for some time, with mixed success, Tim paid her a surprise visit. She answered the door in a pair of shorts. By his own account, Brother Tim spun on his heel, walked right back out the sidewalk to his car, and drove away. The woman who first told me this story chuckled with admiration for Tim's resolve. But the chuckle was double-edged; it also conveyed condescending pity for this woman who didn't know enough to slip into a skirt and save her soul.

The idea of an unannounced inspection struck me as goofy as it was creepy. But that paled in comparison to the idea of this man filled with such vindictive hubris that he was willing to risk this woman's soul to Hell, to abandon her in her own home, willing to stand before the throne of God on the Big Day and say, Lord, she was clad in shorts, so I turned away. I got her behind me, back there with Satan.

I can still see him, down at the south end of the long cookhouse table, right across from me, his big frame backlit in the window, telling this story with booming certitude, and I remember thinking, if the kingdom of heaven can swing on a pair of hot pants, if the cut of your shorts can shift the firmament, then we got trouble. And now, when I think back, I feel a little sorry for him, sad that he could tell these stories in front of a kid like me and not have any perception of my perception. Blown up in his own spiritual bulk, he unwittingly blocked the one true light, and a shadow fell on my heart. In time, I came to know others like Tim Copper. In their zeal to count heads, they lost track of souls. And when they saw some of us turn away, they assumed we simply strayed, or were tempted away, or left in ignorance, when in truth, many of us left in full awareness, seeking a purer truth. He wasn't the only one. But I remember that Sunday. For the first time, I felt the foundation of my faith crack.

On Mondays, we left the Sunday world, and dove back into work. In the weeks leading up to Brother Tim's gospel in the granary, we had been branding. Branding days usually began with a roundup. Understand: When I showed up at the Double 8 Ranch in Elk Mountain, Wyoming, I was no cowboy. I was wearing blue corduroy pants and a flowered disco shirt. It was only my second-favorite disco shirt, but it had flowers on it, and I figured these ranchers I was meeting would be more receptive to flowers than the jarring black and orange geometrics of my number one favorite disco shirt. I was 16, and I had ideas about these things.

I had never ridden a horse. Well, I had, but never really on my own, or to any useful end. There was this neighbor girl once, she was 18, I was 12 or so, and I had for her a saturating case of puppy love, and once, at the pitch of my fever, she gave me a ride on her horse. I remember tingling and trying not to tremble, or trembling and trying not to tingle, and I remember acting desperately nonchalant, but I do not remember the horse, except that I suppose it might have been brown. Then my friend Reno Norsk had a pony named Daisy. He brought her over one day and shared his thermos of sugary iced tea and we rode her out to the swamp, and, because we had heard high schoolers taking about it, we got naked and went streaking. A buddy from high school, George Brux, whom I always remember fondly when I look at the disfigured half-moon under the nail of my right index finger — he flattened it with a racquetball racquet — sent me out on his horse once, and I should have known better, because Georgie was one gleefully sadistic cat, and before it was over the horse was on a runaway. I was dangling by one leg and one arm, just like a movie Indian attacking a Conestoga. I don't remember how we got the horse stopped, but I remember Georgie cackling maniacally. My Grandpa had horses; I think he might have taken me for a ride once. And I had this high-school girlfriend for awhile, we'd ride double out into the moonlight, the horse's hooves whispering through the damp alfalfa, and I'd murmur in her ear and keep my arms around her, and we wafted from one Teen Romance Hall of Fame moment to another, until I reached to open a gate, slid from behind the saddle and landed flat on my back, where I lay gasping like a guppy in the Gobi.

The point is, when I showed up at the Double 8, my horse-riding skills were those of an Eskimo hairdresser. I got away with this for the first two years, since I was only on hire for the haying season. But the third year I came out early for branding season and had to saddle up with the real hands. I learned how to put the saddle blanket on, checking it for any burrs or wrinkles that might cause a saddle sore. I learned about bridles and hackamores, and how to trick a horse into accepting the bit. I was given a saddle, and learned how to cinch it up and strap it down. Some horses fight the cinch, huff up full of air, holding it until you're done, hoping you won't notice. Then they exhale and leave the cinch dangerously slack. When you catch a horse doing this, you knee them in the belly, hard, and when they woof out the air, you snub that cinch up snug as a barrel strap.

I learned, but I just never felt comfortable around horses. For one thing, the other cowboys had been doing this all their lives, and it was impossible for me to replicate their natural ease. They'd see me being tentative, and one of them would say something about acting smarter than the horse. Don't let them know you're afraid of them, that sort of thing. Which is fine, unless you're afraid of them. And I was. Not in a skittery, weak-Willy way, but in a contemplative *My, look at the size of those murderous hocks* way. I grew up around giant Holstein cows, including ones that tried to kick me when I milked them, but acting smarter than a milk cow and acting smarter than a horse are completely separate propositions. And horses, they always look at you with a certain malevolent disdain. Even when you're up in the saddle, reins firmly in hand, a horse can emit palpable rays of contempt simply by adjusting the angle of its ears. They're faster than we, they're sleeker than we, they're hung better than we, and they seem to know it.

In a way, I'm shortselling myself. In all my years on the ranch, I was never bucked off, and I did ride some buckers. Well, one. I learned to slouch into the sway when the horses were walking, I learned how to ride the every-other hippity-bippity groove of a horse on the trot, and I loved to cut out across the prairie after a galloping stray. And my proudest achievement? I never — *never* — grabbed the saddle horn when things got dicey. Only a nancy greenhorn grabs the saddle horn, and I would have sacrificed my sacroiliac before I'd have grabbed the saddle horn in front of all those real cowboys. Of course, it helped that I spent the bulk of my horseback time aboard a one-eyed ball of fire named Cisco.

Cisco was held in reserve for amateurs. He had the disposition of a cranky tortoise, meaning he sustained all the haughty nature of his equine peers, without the sudden moves. I could do just about anything — sneeze, drop my reins or hat — and he would remain stoic, waiting patiently for the incompetent nincompoop on his back to gather up his gear. Apart from the one nonfunctioning walleye, he was in generally good health, and able to perform passably — albeit perfunctorily — in the field. At least, he was able to perform up to the standards I set. I came to feel a measure of affection for Cisco over the years, and even though I knew I was astride the official horse with training wheels, it didn't stop me from slouching and squinting just like all the other cowboys as we headed up the meadow each day to gather the day's branding stock. I may have been riding with training wheels, but by heck, I was riding.

Then came graduation day. Someone else showed up whose horse-riding abilities were worse than mine. As I recall, it was some fair-skinned citified friend of the family on a lark. "What'll we do with Mike?" asked the boss's son. "Put'im on Warts," said the boss.

My boss, the sawed-off, jut-jawed personification of a dyspeptic banty rooster, was a solid and fair man, but he possessed a lurking wild-eyed temper accessed by a fuse shorter than his little bow legs. When the fuse lit, he was prone to sputtering, high-octane tirades. His anger burned bright, but it burned brief. There would be an explosion, a lovely pyrotechnic spray with plenty of boom-boom-boom, and then, just as quickly, silence — the better in which to contemplate the reverberations of his declarations.

"Put'im on Warts," he said, and the adventure began. Warts was a good bit taller than Cisco, lean and deep chestnut brown, and the minute I stepped beside her in the stall, her ears flattened and she began emitting palpable contempt rays. No one told me at the time, but Warts was a head-tosser. That is, in addition to saddle and bridle, she required a piece of equipment, called a tie-down, that ran from her chin to her chest. Without the tie-down, she responded to the reins by tossing her head in the air and shaking her neck. Without the tie-down, she was unsteerable and unstoppable. When I saddled up, I left the tie-down hanging on the tackroom wall.

I led Warts out the stable door, where all the other cowboys and horses were gathered. Several of the hands were fussing over Cisco and the city slicker. I smiled indulgently. No more tenderfoot pony rides for me. Let the Boy Scouts ride that old bag of bones. I tightened the cinch and squinted against the sun. I'm a cowpuncher, baby. I'm a bona-fide, rootin'-tootin' brushpopper on a rootin' tootin' brushpoppin' mo-chine. With one last smug glance at the pasty tourist, I swung aboard.

Perhaps I should say, swung halfway aboard. For as it turned out, my bona-fide, rootin'-tootin' brushpoppin' mo-chine was actually a bona-fide, rootin'-tootin' rocket sled. Just as my foot was about to clear the saddle, that horse ignited.

I've seen drag racing cars that can throw fire 30 feet into the air and burn rubber halfway down a quarter-mile track — this horse made them look like a Rambler with bad clutch plates. My head snapped back, my adrenal glands liquefacted, and my life may have flashed before my eyes, but I couldn't be sure, since the calving shed flashed past at the same time. I sawed on the reins as if I were trying to bring a stampeding water buffalo to heel: Warts just tossed her head back and grabbed another gear. All across that rock-studded field, I sawed, and that horse speed-shifted — whinnying, tossing her head and shaking her mane like Lady Godiva sprinting through boot camp. We just kept gaining speed. I began to imagine I could see a cusp of air before us, bending and whitening as we pushed toward the speed of sound.

And then I saw the fence. Dead ahead, strung high and tight — an endless stretch of five-foot high barbwire. Warts was on course for impact, and showed no signs of slowing. If she hit the fence, she'd be lacerated horribly. I'd probably be thrown clear, but would collect my own unique set of deceleration injuries, the type incurred when one terminates atmospheric re-entry with a headfirst dive into an assortment of tortoise-sized boulders. If she jumped the fence, my end result would likely remain unchanged. And so I took a stupendous breath, slammed my heels into the stirrups, and rared back on the reins like a man trying to shift the Sphinx. If I had yanked on those reins any harder, that horse and I would have journeyed backward in time. The rocks flew, the grass came loose in great clods, and that nag turned her truck around in the space it would take a tree toad to tapdance.

And shot back across the pasture like an asteroid.

I don't remember much about the trip back. Except for the part about did I have clean underwear on, and if you scream will a horse detect fear? I couldn't see too well, as we were roaring right back through the vapor trail we left on the way out. Next thing I remember we skidded smack into the middle of Pres and the rest of the crew. Somebody grabbed the bridle, and somebody grabbed a stirrup. I grabbed my chest. Pres ran to my side, reaching up to help me down. "GET THAT BOY DOWN OFFA THERE!" he yelled. Of course he's upset, I thought. He nearly lost his best hand.

"HE'S A-GONNA RUIN THAT DANG HORSE!"

I say I left the church, but I suppose the departure is necessarily incomplete. My Christian upbringing provides me with a foundation, I suppose, or a sort of sketchy paradigm, but the shining certainties are long gone, corrupted by details. We finance our journey for truth by pawning off our purities, using the wages of sin to purchase insights unavailable to those who choose to remain cloaked in the robes of the true believer. I'm not fool enough to think I've discovered truth. I know better than to rely on my interpretation of anything, be it the gospel or the weather or *Sergeant Pepper's*. I talk about the search for truth, but it is a fool's pursuit.

The more you look, the less you know, to paraphrase Lao-Tsu. My travels have shown me so many believers — leftists, rightists, Buddhists, Muslims, televangelists, crystal-worshipers, and so on — and shown me how many of these same people are sincere and kind and misguided and difficult, that I am left spiritually schizophrenic. There is only one truth, and it is infinitely complex.

Nothing was complex in the granary that hot, late-June evening. There was Brother Tim and the one thunderous truth, and there was a brown-eyed girl two rows over. Two choices. Brother Tim had the stage, and the sound system, and the raging heavens, but that girl had just the breath of a ringlet furled at the lobe of her left ear, and lips like twin strips of silk. I looked at Tim, and for the first time I can recall, realized that all that thunder might just be thunder. I looked at that girl and I saw gentleness, and peace, and the hint of a smile, and I looked back at Tim and I saw bluster and thought maybe he'd soon be belching molten slag, and all I could think of is how that girl's hand would feel in mine. We'd been sneaking around a little bit already. The night before we watched the sun set over the peaks of Sybille Canyon, which were 50 miles away but still visible across the Chugwater Flats. According to local lore, the name Chugwater dated back to the time when Native Americans stampeded buffalo over a nearby cliff into a stream below. The buffalo hit the water with a *chug*. I don't know if the story is true. Someone showed me the cliff once.

The girl was half Native American. It never occurred to me to ask from which tribe. She was smart, and delicate, and strong. Later, when she married a jet engine mechanic in Kansas six months after our last date, I wrote horribly adoring poetry about her, filled with hackneyed references to her ethnicity, including made-up names intended to sound Native American. Horrendous. Verses about her "keeping a tepee with another paleface," equating her "braided raven strands" to a headdress and her denim tennies to moccasins, and lines casting her as "cousin to the wind."

Yikes. But tonight everything was poetic on its own, thick with color and possibility. That hunger-making wind kept pushing under the door, and through the rectangular window panels I could see miles of wheat, orange-drenched and sinuous beneath the billowing octopus-ink sky, the fat gusts pressing the full heads down, making them bow and sway like a vast tribe of slim, trancing pagans.

Still, there was drama within the clean-swept granary as well. Because Brother Tim was winding things up. And because it was Saturday night, he'd be testing the meeting. This is when you find out if the Lord has been moving about in the unsaved souls of the assembled. Brother Tim had laid it all out, let us know what we were in for, and now he would give those who hadn't yet made their choice the opportunity to leave the wickedness of the world — and hot pants — behind. Toward the end of his sermon, he toned it down, became a bit more cajoling. I can't quote him, it's been too long. But having vividly detailed the twists and turns of the path to Hell, having tripped through the nooks and crannies of the fiery pit, he now made a counter-offer. Avoid all this, he said, find your shelter in the Lord, simply by standing to your feet on the last verse of our closing hymn. Make the choice for Christ, choose to walk in the path of righteousness, so that when that final day comes, you will be chosen to stand at the right hand of God.

The place gets electric when the meetings are tested. Grown men shake and weep. Brash youths rise to their feet, faces stained with tears, their soul positively naked with holy humiliation. The buildup to that final verse is unbearable. Even thinking about it now, my chest gets light and edgy, and my pulse lifts. All that preaching, and then, in the space of six or so *a cappella* lines, you find out if any of it took. We finished the chorus, headed into the first lines. Heads swivel. Has anyone risen? Brother Tim lifts his eyes from his hymnal, sweeps the crowd as he did before, only now his eyes have cooled. Heat replaced with hope. The singing falls off a bit, what with everyone rubbernecking, but comes right back. No one is standing. Brother Tim keeps singing and searching. The words scale by and he becomes more furtive, more desperate. There are no histrionics, just subtle shadings. And this isn't about his ego. I believe his fear is true; he doesn't fear that his *tour de force* will go unrewarded, he fears that souls are being lost. The verse is drawing to a close. We're headed for the final chorus. Eternal salvation, going once, going twice . . .

If you want to look good at a branding, you got to have yourself a good heeler man. You got to know that when you arch your back, flip that dogie and free-fall to your knees bear-hugging 200 pounds of bawling, head-butting bull calf, somewhere in there your heeler shot his arm out, snapped his fingers shut on the calf's left rear hoof, yanked straight back with all he had, and hit the dirt butt-first, with his left foot jammed in the back of the calf's right hamhock, driving it forward so the two legs form a splayed "V". Meanwhile, the horse at the other end of the lariat should maintain a steady pull, keeping the loop taut. If the heeler does his job, and if the cowboy on the horse does his, their opposing efforts should anchor the calf between them. Either one lets up, you've got yourself a frantic lapful of beef, thrashing like a bathtub-sized trout with hooves. And if you are timid, or tentative, if you don't dive into that calf like you're twisting up and taking down a speed-freaked halfback, you'll find yourself flat on your back, tasting hot tooth chips and tonguing the gouge in your cheek.

It's a sweaty, smoky, stinky business, branding. It's like football without pads, it's like wrassling in high-heeled shoes. It's hard on cows, hard on cowboys, and hard on animal-rights activists. It is a noisy spectacle in an unforgiving arena. And when you're a kid among strangers, it's a test you can't walk away from. All those cowboys, all that creased leather, the noise, the smoke, your only option would be to walk off into the sagebrush, and then where would you go? Back to your bunk? Out to the dusty county road, to stick out your thumb, catch a ride to the interstate? Nope, you grab the rope and get in there.

I'm a header. I wear one leather glove on my right hand, and when the horse comes at me, towing a bawling calf, I slip past the horse's right flank, dipping in behind the stirrup, and grab the rope — stiff and rough as a frayed oak branch — loosely in my right hand. Stepping quickly now, I run my hand down its taut length until my fist snubs up against the calf's neck. The minute my fist hits, I swing my hips up against the calf's ribcage, reach my left arm across and over the calf's burred spine and down to the left flank, grab the web of skin between the abdomen and upper leg, and then hoist. It all has to happen at once: Hoist, bend your back, lift straight up with both hands, knee the beast skyward, and then, with a tug at the left flank, roll the calf a quarter-turn in midair, laying him out flat so when we hit the dirt the left side will be exposed to the branding iron. Everything has to happen in one fluid motion. Any break in the momentum, and the calf will kick free.

People can get hurt if a calf breaks loose. We work in three or four clumps, usually with our heads down and our backs turned. In the midst of all the heat and dust and noise, men are running from clump to clump handling knives, syringes and glowing branding irons. A rack of extra irons heats in an open flame. Horses work in and out of the groups, and although they're seasoned, a calf stampeding their underbelly can still cause pandemonium. And so the header and the heeler learn to work together, learn to perform this rough work like two dancers re-enacting a mugging. Drop the calf, twist its head back on its neck, flip the lasso free, and hang on until the branding iron arrives.

I think I can still throw a calf. Putting a brand on God is tougher. And what do I believe? I believe Jean Cocteau was on to something when he said there are truths which one can only say after having won the right to say them. I have to believe that, because that has been my path. I believe that the search for truth follows an arc. You begin with the simple truth of ignorance, proceed to the baffling truth of complexity, and then, perhaps not until after death, end your journey with the true truth — the truth of clarity. I'm not sure the truth of clarity is available on this earth. I've met some who claim it, but they often speak not in terms of struggle, but of revelation, and I am suspicious. I suspect they have taken a shortcut, cutting across from the beginning of the arc to the end. In all likelihood, they overshot, and are right back at the beginning, just in a different shade. Very little in this life is simply revealed. There is usually digging and heavy lifting involved, or some falling down. Winning — in Cocteau's terms — is costly. In the battle for my soul, I believe I won the right to some truth, but may have lost the right to redemption. Or is redemption yet available? I hope so. I pray for it, am desperate for it. Peace, grace, a fresh start . . . how I long for them in the dark hours. It is the great irony of spiritual progression: when I had peace, I didn't need it; now that I do, I can't find it. And yes, I've gone back for a look, but it's not where I left it. I read Emerson too late: "God offers to every mind its choice between truth and repose. Take which you please; you can never have both."

So what lies beyond this troubled life? Heaven? Who can say? Residual faith — hanging in threads from the ghostly paradigm — tells me death leads to some type of sorting, but perhaps not. If there's nothing, there's nothing. If there's punishment, get on with it. If there's redemption, well, humble hallelujahs. If we can customize heaven, I'll place my order now: a beat-up truck, an endless backroad, and Lord, a clear conscience.

I assume there will be some accountability, I just don't know to whom. The best I can do is assume a sort of global, no, a *universal* humility. Not an angry atheism, or passive agnosticism. Nor cynignosticism, if you will. Cynicism is overrated, and far too easy.

In small doses, cynicism — like irony — provides an essential tempering quality. But to wallow in it, and to dismiss things like hope and faith, is cowardly and unoriginal. On the other hand, wide-eyed spiritualism doesn't do much good either. Whenever I encounter someone wafting around discovering beauty in all things, I think of Jacob Needleman: "For someone living an uptight, head-restricted experience, a hot bath can feel extraordinary — but it's not a mystical experience. We live such constricted lives that the slightest triggering of a new vital energy gets labeled 'spiritual'." And so, the best I can offer is an unexciting but honest, "I'm sure there's someone bigger than me in this thing, I just don't know." Call it a spiritual cop-out if you will, but I just want to be on record as saying so. So I can stand there some day and say, I didn't know what was right, but I never said you were wrong.

That won't get me far with Brother Tim.

I don't remember if anyone stood that night in the granary. It seems no one did, but many years have passed. If they did, they stood late. Brother Tim closed with a prayer. A quiet prayer. Heartfelt. A gentle coda to a fevered symphony. I sat with my head bowed, glad to be where I was. Doubt was still running under the radar. While everyone filed out of the benches, headed for the other end of the granary for chatter and hot chocolate, I sidestepped through the people to the girl with the ringlet. We slipped out a side door. She took my hand and we ran off through the dust devils, down the long dirt track that cut west through the wheat fields. Thunder tumbled around the sky, and skeins of lightning stitched the clouds as the storm hove over us.

The perception of truth evolves through small revelations. Old truths decay in the same way. The revelations are rarely thunderous. They are mites you can barely hear, working behind the wood. They are corns of wheat, bits of string. They piggy-back our dreams, or wait in the dirt until the day we hit it face-first. We accrete truth like silt. It hones us like wind over sandstone. Over time, it shifts, regrooves itself, reconfigures our faith. We are never finished. We are provided glimpses, if we'll look, but just as quickly, the perspective shifts, and truth is redrawn at the convergence of a new set of lines.

Truth does not always strengthen us. False truth yields false strength, but the truth of clarity cannot be hunted down or summoned from the heavens. A blinding revelation blinds more than it reveals.

Beware truth that strikes like lightning.

At a slight rise well beyond the buildings, we stopped to turn back, and knowing I might never see her again, I gathered her up in my arms. The first fat raindrops were popping in the dust, and we held each other tight, faces thrown back, souls wide open to the water and the fire, and the wind sent Brother Tim's words spinning through the wheat, blowing them out across Chugwater Flats to mingle with the spent breath of long-dead buffalo. ◄

► About the Author

Michael Perry is a native of rural Wisconsin, where he enjoys smelt feeds and the ready availability of shrink-wrapped string cheese, but remains troubled by a pervasive strain of derisive intolerance reserved for anyone — like himself — who is unable to polka.

**Additonal copies of this book
and other titles by Michael Perry**
are available via **mail-order** (see form below)

or at **<www.sneezingcow.com>**

Most titles are also available at **<amazon.com>**

Your name

Shipping address

Title	Price	Number	Total
Big Rigs, Elvis & The Grand Dragon Wayne	$16.95		
Never Stand behind a Sneezing Cow (humor: live-audio recording on cassette)	$9.95		
Why They Killed Big Boy (essays)	$9.95		
Big Boy Out Loud (audio version of Why They Killed Big Boy on cassette)	$9.95		
		shipping	$2.50
		TOTAL	

Clip this form (or make a copy) and send it,
along with check or money order, to

**Whistlers & Jugglers Press
P.O. Box 1346
Eau Claire, WI 54702-1346**

Please visit **<www.sneezingcow.com>**